OPEN ROAD'S BEST OF

Cuba

by Bruce Morris

OPEN ROAD TRAVEL GUIDES –
designed for the amount of time you *really* have for your trip!

Open Road Publishing

Open Road's new travel guides.
Designed to cut to the chase.
You don't need a huge travel encyclopedia – you need a *selective guide* to steer you right. If you're going on vacation for a few weeks or less, get a guide that brings you the *best* of any destination for the amount of time you *really* have for your trip!

Open Road – the guide you need for the trip you want.

The New Open Road *Best Of* Travel Guides.
Right to the point.
Uncluttered.
Easy.

OPEN ROAD PUBLISHING
P.O. Box 284, Cold Spring Harbor, NY 11724
www.openroadguides.com

Text and Maps Copyright © 2012 by Bruce Morris
- All Rights Reserved -
ISBN 13: 978-159360-140-9
ISBN 10: 1-59360-140-9
Library of Congress Control No. 2010909601

About the Author
Bruce Morris grew up in Miami, and is now a writer and musician. He lives in Oak Ridge, Tennessee and Lake Atitlán in Guatemala. He is also the author of *Open Road's Best of the Florida Keys & Everglades, Best of Panama, Best of Guaremala, Best of Cuba,* and co-author of *Best of Costa Rica.* Visit *www.brucemorris.com,* to learn more about Bruce and view his photos from around the world.

For photo and map credits, turn to page 175.

Contents

1. INTRODUCTION 9

2. OVERVIEW 10

Havana 10
Varadero 10
Santiago 10
Cayo Coco, Cayo Santa Maria, Jardines del Rey 12
Guardalavaca 12
Western Cuba – Viñales, María La Gorda, North Coast 14
Nightlife 14
Architecture 15
Shopping 15
Lodging 17
Food & Eating Out 20
Drink 22
Surfing 23
Fishing 23
Scuba Diving/Snorkeling 24
Bird Watching 25
Beaches 26
Parks 26
Music, Music, Music! 26
Hemingway Stuff 28
Baseball 29
Golf 29

3. ITINERARIES 30

4. HAVANA 33

Havana's Sights 34
Best Sleeps & Eats 41
   Sleeps 41
   Eats 48

Best Shopping   53
Best Nightlife & Entertainment   53
Best Sports & Recreation   59

5. VARADERO   62
Varadero's Sights   63
Best Sleeps & Eats   65
   Sleeps   65
   Eats   69
Best Shopping   70
Best Nightlife & Entertainment   71
Best Sports & Recreation   72

6. SANTIAGO DE CUBA   76
Santiago's Sights   77
Best Sleeps & Eats   81
   Sleeps   81
   Eats   84
Best Shopping   84
Best Nightlife & Entertainment   85
Best Sports & Recreation   88

7. THE NORTHERN CAYS   90
Cayo Largo Sights   114
Best Sleeps & Eats   98
Best Shopping   105
Best Nightlife & Entertainment   106
Best Sports & Recreation   106

8. CAYO LARGO   111
Northern Cay Sights   114
Best Sleeps & Eats   115
   Sleeps   115
   Eats   117
Best Shopping   118
Best Nightlife & Entertainment   118
Best Sports & Recreation   118

9. JARDINES DE LA REINA   122

Jardines de La Reina   123
Best Sleeps & Eats   125
   Sleeps   125
   Eats   126
Best Sports & Recreation   126

10. WESTERN CUBA   129

Jardines de La Reina   123
Viñales   130
   Best Viñales Sights   132
   Best Sleeps & Eats   133
     Sleeps   133
     Eats   135
   Best Shopping   136
   Best Nightlife & Entertainment   136
   Best Sports & Recreation   136
María La Gorda   137
   Best Sleeps & Eats   137
     Sleeps   137
     Eats   138
   Best Sports & Recreation   138
Cayo Levisa   139
   Best Sleeps & Eats   139
     Sleeps   139
     Eats   140

11. PRACTICAL MATTERS   142

Getting to Cuba   142
   Airports & Arrivals   142
   Cruises That Visit Cuba   143
Getting Around Cuba   144
   By Air   144
   By Car & Car Rental   144
   By Taxi   146
   By Bus   148
   By Train   148
Basic Information   149
   Banking & Changing Money   149
   Booking Tours & Activities   150

Business Hours   150
Climate & Weather   150
Consulates & Embassies   151
Customs Information   151
Electricity   152
Emergencies & Safety   153
Health   154
Holidays & Celebrations   154
Etiquette   156
Food & Dining   157
Further Reading   158
Hotels & Lodging   159
Internet Access   160
Language   160
Newspapers & Magazines   160
Maps   161
Postal Service   161
Time   161
Tipping   161
Tourist Information   163
Water   163
Websites   163
Weights & Measures   164
What to Bring   164
Essential Spanish   165
Pleasantries   165
Everyday Phrases   165
Travel Terms   166
Eating & Drinking   166

INDEX   169

Maps

Cuba   11
Havana   37
Varadero   64
Santiago   78
Northern Cays: Cayo Coco, Cayo Guillermo,
Cayo Santa María & Guardalavaca   92
Cayo Largo   113
Jardines de La Reina   124
Western Cuba   131

Open Road's Best Of ...

CUBA!

1. INTRODUCTION

This is the part of the book where I need to convince you, the reader, about the charms of Cuba. It's easy to sell Cuba. I've made a handy list of things about the country that make it so attractive to visitors. The short list includes great beaches, great music, great fishing and diving, great drinking and friendly people. Just read the next chapter and you'll run right out and buy a plane ticket to Cuba immediately.

Cuba packs a lot of punch in a small country. It's about the size of Tennessee or roughly three times the size of Wales. There are **numerous attractions in a small area**, and good transportation infrastructure. Havana is one of the most interesting cities in the world. Great rum, beer, music, beaches, great fishing, diving and water sports make Cuba one of the most interesting countries to visit.

Cuban beaches are famous for powdery white sand and clear water. There are dozens of beachfront all-inclusive, budget resorts to choose from. Travelers from all over the world come for week and two-week long holidays making Cuba one of the Caribbean's top destinations.

2. OVERVIEW

HAVANA
One of the great cities of the world, everyone should try to visit Havana at least once in their life. I love the town. The old part of Havana is a **UNESCO World Heritage Site** and, although old and crumbling, richly deserves the designation. Without doubt, Havana is one of the most fascinating cities in the world. Noisy, crowded, chaotic, dirty, very poor—it's wonderful.

Hot music seems to be coming from every window and doorway. Hanging out on the steps in front of their apartments with a bottle of rum and cards or dominoes is how many Cubans seem to pass a lot of their time. Stop and chat. *Habaneros* are friendly and curious about visitors.

There are so many things for visitors to do in Havana, the city rates a guidebook all to itself. **Music, museums, nightclubs,** and architecture are outstanding. The people are friendly and interested in meeting and talking with foreigners. Most people speak at least a few words of English and you are likely to meet some who are fluent.

VARADERO
With dozens of all-inclusive resorts to choose from, **fabulous white sand beaches** and lots of nightlife, Varadero is Cuba's Cancun but with Canadian, European and Latin American flavor—there is not much US-style spring break action but things are probably more fun without it. With its own international airport and location not too far from Havana, it is easy to get to and many people spend their entire Cuban holiday right in Varadero.

SANTIAGO
Cuba's musical capitol and second largest city, Santiago has a quaint old colonial city center that is the main draw for most visitors. Music lovers should not miss *Casa de La Trova* to hear the best of traditional and modern Cuban music. July **Carnival** in Santiago is one of the best in the Caribbean.

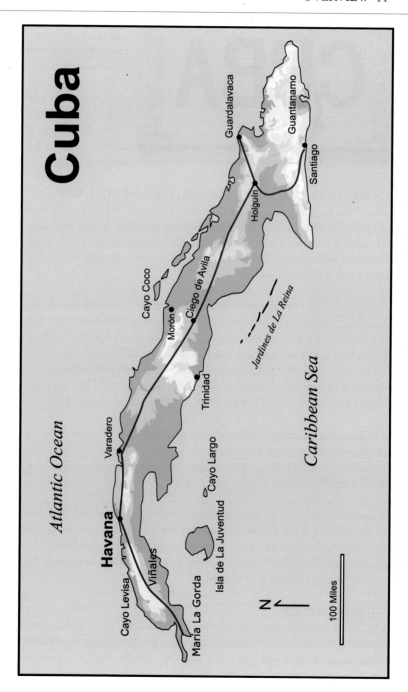

The city and surroundings are home to a plethora of historic sites including the famous **Moncada Barracks** and **Morro Castle**. Architectural marvels seem to be on every block.

CAYO COCO, CAYO SANTA MARIA, JARDINES DEL REY

These islands, "cayos" as they are called in Cuba are on the north coast east of Havana and have some of the finest **beaches** anywhere in the Caribbean. The islands are low, uninhabited and hot with mangroves and scrub. Wild cattle still roam around. The water around them is crystal-clear, warm year round and teems with sea life.

Starting around 1985 the government in partnership with foreign developers built causeways from the mainland to the string of offshore cayos and began building a series of large resorts. They picked a great spot for it. There are now about 30 **sun and sea, beach and buffet, all-inclusive resorts** on the cayos operated by the Cuban government in partnership with some of the world's largest hotel chains: Barceló, Meliá, and Accor. There is a large airport with direct flights from Canada, England and Latin America.

The developments were reasonably well planned from an environmental standpoint but some complain the causeways do not have enough drainage under them and the ecology of the shallow bays is damaged due to blocking of tidal flow.

To keep the cayos nice for tourists, the government does not allow Cubans to actually live there. Resort workers stay for a week at a time in special housing blocks and are bused back and forth to the mainland. The causeways have gates and guards to keep any undesirables away from the money-bringing busloads of tourists.

GUARDALAVACA

On Cuba's northeast coast, yet another beautiful beach destination, many people feel Guardalavaca is Cuba's best. There are several beach and buffet **all-inclusive resorts** and the small town of Guardalavaca is close for exploring. The beaches are certainly stunning. Other than relaxing by the pool or on the beach, fishing, diving and less strenuous water sports are about the only things to do. Contrived-seeming tours to mainland sights are available in the resorts.

CAYO LARGO

Cayo Largo with its modern international airport has some of Cuba's finest beaches and some of Cuba's best **beach and buffet** all-inclusive resorts. The white, powdered sugar beaches go on for miles (*see photo below*). The **fishing and diving** are some of the best in the hemisphere. The island is a short, half-hour flight from Havana and there are direct flights from the UK and Canada.

JARDINES DE LA REINA

Off the southwest side of Cuba are several long chains of islands similar to the Florida Keys but with almost no development whatsoever. 40 miles offshore, Jardines de La Reina, **Gardens of the Queen**, have no development whatsoever—no houses, no marinas, no hotels, no radio masts, nothing. They are now what the Florida Keys must have been like 200 years ago.

The area is famous for its **pristine coral reefs** with scuba diving and fishing unlike anything else in the hemisphere. An Italian company, Avalon, has a license from the government to take small groups of divers and anglers to its floating hotel for exclusive, catch and release trips.

In the early 1950s the government established a large, 840 square mile marine park in the area: *Parque Nacional Jardines de la Reina*. The Cuban park service scrupulously controls the parks and the very efficient Cuban Coast Guard patrols them. There has been no commercial fishing or exploitation in the area whatsoever for over 60 years. This means the sea life is unspoiled, one of the **greatest undersea parks in the world**. See

National Geographic Magazine's February 2002 issue for some stunning photos.

WESTERN CUBA – VIÑALES, MARÍA LA GORDA, NORTH COAST

One of Cuba's most popular and famous destinations, **Viñales** is famous for its exotic landscape of jungle-covered *mogotes*, caves and **tobacco plantations**. It is certainly beautiful and well worth the effort to rent a car or book a bus tour to drive around and take in the sights.

There are only a couple of places to stay suitable for most tourists so be sure to book your lodgings well in advance—you can't just pop in and expect to find a vacant room.

Divers love **María La Gorda** at Cuba's extreme most western point. Bungalows are available right on the palm tree-shaded beach.

At the extreme western end of the island, **UNESCO Biosphere Reserve** and Cuban national park **Guanahacabibes Peninsula** is a birdwatchers paradise.

Cayo Levisa and **Cayo Jutias** are very small islands a short distance off the northwest coast. There is one small resort on each island set right on the beach. They are run down but wonderfully situated. These resorts offer little other than snorkeling and beach walks. I love them.

NIGHTLIFE

Cuba is absolutely, justifiably, wonderfully famous for music and nightlife. If you come for no other reason, you will have traveled well. And not just Havana: Santiago and Trinidad are also justly renowned for excellent music and associated nightlife. From the touristy **Casa de La Música** to the *muy auténtico* **Salón Rosada de Beny Moré**, there are hundreds of hot music venues in every town in Cuba. The government does a good job supporting the arts and the result is a throbbing, lively music and dance scene.

ARCHITECTURE
Havana, Trinidad and Santiago are rich with surviving colonial architecture. While much of Cuba's architectural heritage is crumbling due to lack of restoration funds, the government is making efforts to preserve some of the more interesting colonial facades along Havana's Malecón.

SHOPPING
Now for the bad news. There is really not much to buy in Cuba of interest to visitors other than rum, cigars, coffee and Che t-shirts. Cuba has a rather poor **artisanal crafts** scene although it seems to be improving as the government begins to allow its artisans to work for their own account.

You can purchase **wonderful paintings** but be sure to check if the government will allow you to take them out of the country—the nicest artwork is often confiscated in the airport as you leave. Cuba's heritage should be kept in Cuba seems to be the reason.

On Saturday afternoons on Havana's Prado, dozens of independent artists offer their works for sale on the tree-shaded sidewalk. Some are very, very well done. In my opinion, this is the best of what Cuba has for sale and the artists receive the money directly—it goes straight into their pockets. The government does not get the rake off it usually gets in almost every transaction on the island.

Cigars
Cuban cigars are justly famous and a great gift purchase. Expect to pay upwards of CUC 6 each for good cigars.

Many people will offer to sell you cigars, on the street, in your hotel and in clubs. Most bought outside of an official government cigar store are fakes—some good but most of decidedly inferior quality.

Rum

Cuba is of course justifiably famous for its rum. **Havana Club, Santiago** and **Varadero** are the best known but you will see a wide variety of other brands for sale. Locals buy cheap stuff in bottles with no label for about US$ 0.05 a liter. Dark, smoky rums make great presents or additions to your own liquor cabinet back home. The problem I have is, if my friends know I have a bottle of Cuban rum in the house, they won't leave until they know it's all gone. Be sure to pack the rum in your checked bags as it may be confiscated changing planes if you try to carry it in your hand baggage.

Cigar-Smuggling Tourists

Be aware that the government forbids buying or selling of any cigars outside of the official stores and considers anyone attempting to take any cigars not purchased in an official, government-run store out of the country to be smugglers. So don't buy cigars from guys on the street unless you are going to smoke them in Cuba.

Coffee

Cubita coffee is available all over the island. A kilo of beans usually goes for CUC 4. This is a great buy since you can't get it back in the US and the dark, dark flavor works really well with espresso/cappuccino machines. I love it.

Guayaberas

I like guayaberas. You will see old guys wearing these comfortable, not tucked into the trousers shirts and may be tempted to buy a couple for yourself. They can be casual and formal at the same time. You can wear them on almost any occasion. But realize that only old guys wear them anymore. Young people prefer t-shirts with cool slogans or sport shirts with little alligators on them.

Since Cuba has almost no textile industry, most of the guayaberas you see for sale in Cuba are of poor quality or imported from Spain, Mexico or England. The ones actually made in Cuba are usually constructed from old bed sheets stolen from hotels.

You can buy nice, imported guayaberas in the gift shop on the mezzanine level of the **Hotel Parque Central**.

If you want a really nice guayabera made from the best Irish linen, Ramón Puig at La Casa De Las Guayaberas on Calle Ocho in Little Havana in Miami does a great job. They are not cheap. *Info*: *www.mycubanstore.com*.

The best guayaberas in the world come from Edgar Gomez in Cartagena, Columbia. He custom makes them for rock stars, presidents, dictators and the like and they will last you all your life. You can leave them to your kids when you die. The guy speaks no English. *Info: Calle Portobelo 10 - 92 San Diago, Cartagena de Indias, Colombia. Tel. 57-300-805-8753.*

LODGING
Cuba is rapidly adding to its 53,000 rooms mostly by collaborating with European and South American hotel companies like Meliá and Accor. Even the very best Cuban hotels do not compare well with hotels in the rest of the world. In some areas of the country I am unable to give a hearty recommendation for any place to stay. In those areas, I will describe what I have seen and let you make the decision.

There are a few standout hotels and resorts but don't expect anything, anywhere in Cuba, to distantly approach an actual five-star lodging. Comfortable and clean can be had, good service and good food are more difficult. The star system in Cuba promulgated by the government bears no resemblance to any star-rating system anywhere else in the world. If you

Cuba Facts

Location:	Caribbean/Atlantic
Land Area:	42,800 sq mi, about the same size as Tennessee
Highest Point:	6,578 feet (2005 m)
Population:	12 million
Climate:	Tropical
Biodiversity:	6,522 plant species, +/- 368 bird species, 59 mammal species
Languages:	Spanish, English, Russian
Literacy:	95%
Life Expectancy:	76 men, 80 women
Poverty Rate:	Unknown, but average salary is $20/month
Government:	Communist/Fidelismo
Independence:	1902 (Cuban Government dates independence to 1959 Revolution)
Economy:	State-controlled, GDP: $111 billion

subtract two stars you will be getting close to the actual international rating level. Ratings of hotels within Cuba can be wildly uneven.

Rooms in government-approved private homes, *casas particulares*, can be a very good, economical choice for the slightly more adventurous. I list some of the most interesting ones in the *Best Sleeps* sections.

Hotels

The Cuban government is owner or majority partner in almost all lodging in the country. Tourism efforts concentrate on mass-tourism—the government prefers the type of tourists who travel in large groups on buses moving together from plane to hotel to group tour back to the resort again. Most of the resorts in the beach areas are built from the ground up with this type of tourism in mind. Many, many resorts in Cuba operate on an all-inclusive basis.

Traveling around on your own, booking hotels casually from night to night from place to place can be done but independent travel is harder and much more expensive in Cuba than in most other countries. Hotels charge fixed, top prices to walk-ins. Rooms booked in advance, from out of the country in a package are routinely half of what you pay if you just walk up to the check-in desk and ask for a room. There are no hostels and there is not really much of a backpacker circuit.

Recently an effort has been made to create what in Cuba passes for "boutique" hotels. **Los Frailes** in the old part of Havana is a good example. These can be nice but need to be booked well in advance and can be expensive. Government-run **Habaguanex Hotels** has developed and manages some higher-end lodging although their name attached does not guarantee a nice hotel by any means.

Casas Particulares

Rooms in government-approved private homes, *casas particulares*, can be a very good, economical choice for the slightly more adventurous. I list some of the most interesting ones in the *Best Sleeps* sections.

One of the particularly good uses for this book is as a guide to the best hotels in each area. I have tried to identify the best ones in each part of the country by actually sleeping in them and by keeping in touch with other guests and travelers. Also, I keep up with several web sites (listed in *Practical Matters)* that are useful for selecting places to stay.

The problems with most of the hotels and other tourist services in Cuba include **disinterested employees.** Service can be slow, rude or non-existent. Hotel food is, in general rather poor. A few of the nicer hotels can come up with good meals but they are exceptions and will usu-

ally be extremely expensive. **Maintenance can be sadly lacking.** Many rooms in a resort may be unavailable due to cannibalizing for hard-to-come-by spare parts.

All-Inclusive Resorts
The bulk of tourism to Cuba is to the numerous all-inclusive beach and buffet resorts. Most are partnerships with international hotel chains such as Meliá, Barceló and Accor. Many are located on Cuba's wonderful beaches and are frequented by snowbirds from England, Canada, Russia, and Europe and, in the southern hemisphere's winter, Argentina, Brazil and Chile.

The resorts feature **colossal buffets** with prepared dishes, meats, cheeses, fruits, pastry selections, ice cream, grill stations, pizza selections and much, much more. Quality of the food at the buffets can vary from resort to resort. The buffets are usually large enough for even the fussiest eater to find something that suits them.

Lodging Prices
Prices quoted are for one double room for two people.

$	Backpacker: non-existent
$$	Budget: $25-75
$$$	Midrange: $75-150
$$$$	First-class: $150-300
$$$$$	Luxury: $300 and up

The all-inclusive beach & buffet resorts can be real bargains—**one of the few bargains in Cuba.** Packages including airfare, transfers, all food and unlimited alcoholic beverages can be purchased for under $100 per night for a couple.

FOOD & EATING OUT

In spite of the negative things I am about to say below, **you can enjoy wonderful food** in Cuba. You can have great dining experiences in most parts of the country. **Unfortunately, you have to work a little** to find great food. I try to do most of that work for you and describe some good restaurant choices. Bring your own hot sauce with you.

My friends from the States, the ones who haven't been to Cuba, tell me how much they love hot, spicy Cuban food. Other than a grocery store Cuban sandwich, rarely anything other than a regular old ham and cheese submarine, grinder, hoagie, they haven't actually tried any Cuban food. Cuban restaurants in the US benefit from something that is not happening in Cuba: a wide variety of easily obtainable ingredients, and the incentive to prepare and serve top-quality, interesting food—absolutely unlike the dining scene in Cuba.

So here's the real deal: Cuban food in Cuba is **almost always bland**, un-spiced, over- or undercooked and often served cold. That's it. Sorry. It sucks. Over many trips to the island I can count on the fingers of one hand the number of times I have seen hot peppers. I have eaten with Cuban families, in fancy restaurants, in crummy restaurants, the very fanciest hotels available, in shabby street stalls and have *never* had what I would call a spicy meal. Pork, chicken and fish, pasta and pizza are the staples and are usually served, extremely well done, dry and often, cold. Be prepared for not-very-interesting meals.

The government runs almost all restaurants in Cuba and staff earns in the area of US$1 per day. This leads to lack of motivation, bored cooks, unsanitary food preparation, indifferent-to-rude wait staff, overcharging, and scams. Most restaurants and bars seem to be running an off the books deal wherein employees share out on a pre-determined basis whatever income they can keep off the official books.

Most complaints about food in the all-inclusive resorts revolve around cleanliness and hygiene. Open air dining means lots of flies and birds sharing the buffet.

There is almost always a 10% "*servicio*" or service charge added to your check. This is NOT a tip. It is a tax disguised as a tip. The money goes straight to the government and the wait staff and other restaurant employees receive none of it. If you want to reward good service you should add at least 10% on top of the total bill—in cash.

Paladars

Wait! There is one major exception! The very few privately run restaurants allowed by the government, called paladars, *paladares*, are usually good to excellent dining experiences. Usually located in peoples' homes with only a few tables, the owners actually try to serve good food. They know the word about the quality of their food will get around, more people will come and they will earn more money. *Paladars* are highly regulated and taxed so don't expect bargains but you can find some wonderful meals.

Officially, *paladars* are allowed to have only one room with four tables with no more than 16 seats, no employees (only family members may participate) and are heavily inspected, regulated and taxed. In reality, families with good connections to high-ranking government officials slide by and some are running quite nice, upscale eateries with dozens of tables, great wine lists and creative menus. *Paladars* are usually the best choice for lunch or dinner. A few are not much better than the government run restaurants but, if you want to eat well, paladars are the best way to go.

Mostly only **sad street food** is available so don't get too excited. Pizza is usually poor quality with a smear of tomato sauce and a hint of cheese on a tough piece of dough. Spam sandwiches are one of the most common street food choices. Wonderful strong, sweet Cuban coffee is available at street side windows for around US$0.05. Watery ice cream is a popular street food. CUCs are usually accepted but if you have some Cuban pesos you can eat for pennies.

Most *casas particulares* will prepare food for guests or other foreigners if arranged in advance. Eating this way, in a Cuban home, you have an excellent chance of having a wonderful meal.

Restaurant Prices

$	$5 or less
$$	$5-$8
$$$	$8-$12
$$$$	$12-$25
$$$$$	Over $25

Light or Dark?

Mojitos, daiquiris and other mixed rum drinks with fruit are usually better when made with light rum. The heavy flavor of the dark rums can overpower the mixers. Proper bartenders should be hesitant to mix fine aged rum with anything. The old stuff is for sipping straight or, perhaps, on the rocks (*con hielo, por favor*).

DRINK

Cuba has numerous, excellent rums and several good beers. Most North American pop is expensively available. Coke, Pepsi and Sprite appear on many menus. Local equivalents such as *Tucola* are cheaper and generally a little sweeter than their US counterparts. Wait staff will frequently insist on serving you the imported, more expensive US brands.

Beer

Cuban beer is generally quite good. The best brands, **Hatuey** (rarely actually available) and **Bucanero** are, in my opinion, great. **Cristal** is weak, thin and gassy. More expensive Corona, Becks and Heineken are sometimes available.

Rum

Cuban rums are the stars of the show. World famous **Havana Club, Santiago** and **Varadero** are always good choices. I generally prefer dark, aged rum, called *añejo*. You will see rum aged for three years, five years, and seven years or even longer. The older, the smokier, the more flavor. I find the older rums to be a bit too sweet for me, with a vanilla flavor. My favorite tipple: **Santiago Añejo** aged for three years.

Now, after the big build-up, let me tell a story that may change your mind about Havana Club rum. One day while walking along Neptuno in Havana, I passed an open doorway and glanced inside to see a very large, dark room filled with dozens of long folding tables. On the tables were hundreds of empty Havana Club bottles. A guy with a 55-gallon steel drum on wheels was filling the bottles from the drum using a ladle and funnel. Was this the official Havana Club bottling plant? I don't think so. Were they filling the bottles with real Havana Club? I don't think so.

Wine

Wines imported from Chile, Argentina and Spain are widely available and generally good. If you are unsure which to choose, keep in mind that almost any Spanish wine listed as *crianza* or *reserva* will be superb.

SURFING

Cuba is pretty much uncharted territory for surfers with rumors and legends of major, unsurfed breaks. It is not a major surf destination by any means but there are good quality waves in the right season.

The best surf is mostly on the eastern part of the island from September through December. The best surf happens when large tropical storms are approaching the island or passing to the south.

Yumuri, Rio Duaba, Playa Mar Verde, Bella Pluma and **Verraco** are the best-known spots. Check out www.havanasurf-cuba.com for more information.

FISHING

Fishing in Cuba is some of the best in the world. There are several reasons for this: warm, tropical waters, the nearby Gulf Stream and very little fishing pressure. Few Cubans are allowed to use boats and there are not many government-run commercial fishing operations. So the locals are not out there hoovering up anything in the sea that moves like in most countries.

Cuba suffers from almost no poaching from international factory-fishing fleets since, unlike most Latin American countries, Cuba maintains a vigorous, serious and viable coast guard. All mariners know it is a very bad thing to be picked up by the Cuban coast guard so the rogue factory fishing boats steer clear.

Almost immediately after the 1959 revolution, Cuba established several large marine national parks and closed them to commercial fishing and exploitation. Their pristine nature has been fastidiously protected since then. A few are open to very limited, catch-and-release sport fishing. And it is astoundingly good fishing.

There is good fishing all over the island. Organized trips are available in almost all resort areas. Usually charter trips must be booked in advance from outside Cuba.

Where to Fish?

The northwest coast is best for bill fishing in the Gulf Stream. The south and west sides of the island offer some of the best fishing for bonefish, tarpon, permit and reef species anywhere in the hemisphere. **Los Jardines de La Reina, Cayo Coco** and **Isla de La Juventud** are the top destinations.

Inner Tube Fishing!

For serious, hard-core fishermen, nothing tops the inner tube guys in Havana. Since the government allows very few boats and most of the small boats have been stolen for trips to Miami, you will see these young fishermen wearing only shorts with huge inner tubes along the Malecón setting out with hand lines for a day's fishing. They also free dive with very basic spears and simple goggles. They go *waaay* out in these contraptions.

Unfortunately, many of the best spots are difficult to reach without spending large amounts of money. The Cuban government controls everything, including tourist-fishing trips. The few Cuban fishing lodges are very well run, comfortable, serve wonderful food and are not really more expensive than comparable lodges in Central or South America. They are well equipped with good skiffs and fairly new tackle. **Avalon**, an Italian company, runs a top-notch operation in several locations.

Fishing for **largemouth bass** in Cuba is just about the best there is anywhere—Arkansas included. Cuba sports more than 21 known bass lakes and catches of over 100 bass per day of up to ten pounds are not unusual. Many bass in the 20 lbs.-range have been reliably reported and it is likely that the next world record, over 25 lbs. bass will come from Cuba. The government protects the lakes and several have been designated catch and release only for many years.

Lake **Hanabanilla**, **Laguna Redonda** near Cayo Coco and **Florencia** reservoir in Ciego de Avila province are some of the top bass destinations.

SCUBA DIVING & SNORKELING
I can confidently tell you that the diving in Cuba rivals that of any of the top Caribbean dive locations: Honduras's Bay Islands, the Cayman Islands or Belize. I am constantly amazed at the numbers and size of the fish I see wherever I dive in Cuba.

The reasons for this are the same as for why the fishing is so good: large, protected marine parks, few local fishermen, a very small commercial fleet and vigorous enforcement of Cuba's fishing laws.

The top spots are the remote **Jardines de La Reina** on the south side of the island and the reserves around **Cayo Largo**. The diving is simply some of the best anywhere. *National Geographic* published a feature on the area in the February 2002 issue.

Other top spots include **María La Gorda, Cayo Levisa** and **Santiago**.

Unfortunately, many visitors to the island come away with a lesser opinion of Cuba's diving opportunities. Most Cuban resorts are all-inclusive with highly organized activities for guests and organize snorkeling and scuba trips the same way they do all their touristy activities—herding visitors around like cattle.

Snorkelers in these types of resorts almost always outnumber scuba divers so divers are not always taken to the best spots for scuba. Dive boats are usually not willing to run far to the best spots but concentrate on the same two or three spots closest to the resort. Most dive operations in Cuba are in resorts and operated for common tourists rather than for serious, experienced scuba divers.

There are several locations with top-quality dive operations and pristine reefs. **Jardines de La Reina** and **Cayo Largo** are served by the very professional Italian company Avalon which has excellent equipment, boats and guides.

Don't be surprised when a very serious, fully outfitted soldier, complete with machine gun, climbs on board the boat for your dive trip. He is there to make sure your dive boat captain does not decide to hightail it to Miami. Another soldier stays on shore and watches your entire trip through binoculars so he can alert the Cuban Coast Guard if the dive boat makes any suspicious moves.

BIRD WATCHING

With 368 species including 26 endemic species, Cuba is rapidly becoming a birding destination for both serious and casual birders. Talented guides are available in some resorts. Western Cuba and the swamps to the south are prime areas for spotting such beauties as *Cuban green woodpecker, Fernandina's flicker, bee hummingbird, Cuban pygmy-owl,* or even a *Cuban gnatcatcher.*

BEACHES

How do I describe what I think are some of the nicest beaches in the Caribbean? It's not easy to do. Cuba has wonderful, wonderful beaches. Powdery white sand, gentle waves, miles long, there are simply hundreds of beauties to choose from.

The all-inclusive resorts front on some of the nicest beaches but even in the most touristy beach areas you can find miles and miles of deserted beaches to wander on. For many, Cuba's beaches are the reason for the trip with rum and music distant seconds. I can understand this.

Perhaps the nicest of them all, **Playa Sirena** and **Playa Paraíso** in Cayo Largo are powdered sugar—white and fluffy with clear water and usually mild surf. Varadero and the northern cayos also have beautiful white sand beaches.

PARKS

Cuba is filthy with national parks and preserves. Several offshore marine parks protect vast swaths of coral reefs. Many of the parks have been in place for over 50 years and visiting the environments they protect is like using an ecological time machine. There are **10 World Heritage Sites** and **six Biosphere Reserves**.

Caguanes National Park near Cayo Coco is easily visited from the nearby beach resorts. There are organized excursions from Havana to **Viñales Valley** (*see photo below*) and the **Guanahacabibes Península** in the western end of the island. **Jardines de la Reina** is a string of islands about 40 miles off the south coast of Cuba, probably akin to what the Florida Keys must have been like 200 years ago. The reef systems are well-protected and in great shape.

MUSIC, MUSIC, MUSIC!

Cuba rocks. Hot Latin sounds seem to be everywhere. Every corner bar has a live combo wailing out son standards. The **Buena Vista Social Club** lives

on in Casas de La Trova, in bars, nightclubs and resort lobbies. Youthful new musical flavors sprout and grow in the hothouse that is Cuba's music scene. Radio and television offer interesting selections of Cuban pop.

You will hear a wide variety of music which may be lumped together as "Cuban" even though styles may have originated elsewhere. Many of the most popular Latin styles originated in Cuba.

Here is my meager attempt to describe the main styles of music you may hear in Cuba.

Son is experiencing a strong revival partly due to the popularity of the Buena Vista Social Club. It is what most people nowadays would think of as "Cuban music." A typical son group will always include a *tres*—a nylon, six stringed guitar with the strings doubled up close together in three pairs. It has a very distinctive sound kind of like a mandolin or 12-string guitar. **Beny Moré**, the demi-god of son, is considered a holy man to many Cubans. He also had one of the best-known **mambo** bands back in the day. You will hear lots and lots of son but probably not much mambo.

Trova might be compared to US folk music or country music pre Bob Dylan. It is one of the main roots of contemporary Cuban music. **Guantanamera** is the quintessential trova song—very romantic. Enthusiasts should make a pilgrimage to **Casa de La Trova** in Santiago for some rootsy trova or possibly some slightly racier **bolero**.

You may also hear **Nueva Trova** which is perhaps like US folk music *after* Bob Dylan. It could be called Cuban singer/songwriter often performed solo with acoustic guitar—less romance and more protest—often highly patriotic.

Rumba is all about rhythm and features conga drums and percussion instruments. It's pretty high-energy and rootsy with heavy African influence. The dancing can be highly erotic. Try and see **Los Papines**, an oldie but still active group, if you can.

Traditional **Danzón** is fairly formal, entirely instrumental, and orchestral with the addition of congas. Weekend dance sessions can be found in almost every Cuban town. Aficionados tend to be middle-aged and up. Great groups to hear would include **Charanga de Oro** and **Orquesta Barbarito Diez**.

Salsa is less a particular style of music than a name many people use to describe almost any type of fast Latin music. **Los Van Van**, who still perform live in Cuba from time to time, would be a good example of this very modern and very popular style.

Timba is a flavor of salsa particular to the Havana scene. Hot groups you might be able to see include **Los Van Van**, **NG La Banda** and **Haila**.

Cuban Jazz, epitomized by **Chucho Valdez** and **Irakere**, emphasizes percussion instruments, electric piano and brass. The **Jazz Café** in Havana is the place to go for some of the best Cuban jazz acts. All of the greats have played there.

Radio stations and TV music video shows will bombard you with plenty of **Cuban rock**, **Cuban hip-hop**, **reggaeton** and the fashionable-with-the-teens **Cubaton**. You will have trouble getting away from it.

HEMINGWAY STUFF

Great author Ernest Hemingway spent many years living in Cuba and his ghost still haunts a few of his favorite hangouts. Hemingway pilgrimage sites include a couple of nice old bars in Havana: **El Floridita** (the daiquiris are fair; there is a statue of him at the bar – *see photo below*) corner of Obispo y Monserrate, and the charming **La Bodeguita del Medio** (mojitos) on

Empedrado. They are within a couple of blocks of each other and are over-priced and almost always crammed with tourists.

Hard-core fans may want to trek to **Cojímar** near where the Old Man lived with his Cuban first mate, Gregorio Fuentes.

Hemingway lived from time to time in the **Hotel Ambos Mundos** on Calle Obispo for about 10 years and his room is preserved as a shrine. They still have his typewriter. You can drink in the rooftop bar. Nice.

The **Museo Ernest Hemingway**, Finca Vigía, is his former suburban home overlooking Havana. It is nicely kept up and has a good collection of original Hemingway stuff, including his typewriter. His old boat, the Pilar, is preserved on the tennis court. It is definitely worth the taxi ride and small entrance fee.

BASEBALL

El beisbol as it's known in Cuba is truly great. Don't miss it! Cuba currently has 18 national teams in two leagues and the quality of play is some of the best in the world. Aging and rather basic stadiums give the spectator not only a great game to watch but a chance to get up close to the "real Cuba" many visitors are looking to experience.

Most Cubans are ready to talk *beisbol* with you at the drop of a ball cap and can tell you when the next game is. Games cost US$ 0.05 if you have local money and CUC 5 if you have only tourist money. There are no hats or souvenirs for sale but you can usually buy pork sandwiches and *Tucola*.

GOLF

Currently, there are **two golf courses** in the country but, reportedly more are in the works. Don't expect Pebble Beach. Fairways are dusty and dry. The greens need watering.

The Cuban government has announced their intention to build at least 15 new courses in the country in the next five to seven years.

3. ITINERARIES

It is difficult to visit Cuba for just a day or two. A weekend is enough to enjoy Havana or Santiago and most visitors come for a week or more planning to spend a few days in Havana and the rest of their time enjoying Cuba's famous beach and buffet resorts.

Weeks could be spent exploring **Havana** but travelers can certainly see the main sites and soak up plenty of Havana culture in only a two or three day trip. A trip to Cuba would not be complete without at least a night or two in Havana. Most international flights land there but some flights go directly to the beach resorts. If you have time, most of the resorts offer an overnight tour to Havana.

Cuban **beaches** are some of the best in the Caribbean. The government has built clusters of all-inclusive resorts in several locations around the country where the beaches are spectacular and water sports well developed.

If you have **just a couple of days** for your entire Cuba trip, pick either **Havana** or **Santiago**.

If you have **a week** you can explore **Havana** for a few days and then **Viñales** and **María La Gorda** for diving, birding and beach relaxation. Budget at least a week for **Beach & Buffet resorts** or a **live aboard fishing** or **diving** expedition.

With **two weeks** or more you can spend plenty of time in **Havana** and on the **beaches** and still have time to explore **Viñales** or spend a week catching and releasing **bonefish**, **tarpon** and **permit**.

Western Cuba

Drive along the north shore on royal palm-studded northern route through **Mariel**, **Bahía Honda** and **Las Cadenas** to **Viñales**. Marvel at the weird landscape. Head to **María La Gorda** for **scuba diving** and visit the **Guanacahabibes Peninsula** for **birding**. Stop for a few days at **Playa Las**

Tumbas for a very basic and tranquil beach rest. The drive back to Havana could include stops at Pinar Del Rio and San Cristóbal.

Fishing
When anglers think of Cuba, Hemingway and fishing for blue marlin come immediately to mind. Bill fishing in Cuba is excellent but facilities (good boats and marinas) are not well developed. Both Havana and Cayo Coco have marinas and charter boats available.

The best fishing in Cuba by far is off the southwest coast in Los Jardines de La Reina, Cayo Largo and Isla de La Juventud. Fly fishermen catch record numbers of bonefish, tarpon and permit on the miles and miles of pristine flats. Huge marine national parks ensure spectacular fishing. Cayo Largo has the best bone fishing I have encountered anywhere and also has a couple of Cuba's best beach resorts so you can be out fishing in the sun all day and return to enjoy resort-style luxury.

Fishing for largemouth bass is one of Cuba's secret delights. The warm climate and lack of angling pressure mean bass over 10lbs. are common. Many expect the next world record to come from one of Cuba's many lakes. Trips to lakes Hanabanilla, Laguna Redonda and Florencia are popular mostly with visiting US anglers.

Scuba Diving
Diving in Cuba is excellent and the government's dedication to preserving the exceptional conditions of their marine national parks makes for pristine coral and dense marine life. The best diving is off the southwest coast in Los Jardines de La Reina, Cayo Largo, Isla de La Juventud and María La Gorda. Cayo Largo has several of Cuba's best beach resorts so you can combine diving with resort pleasures in one vacation.

Nature, Music & History
Enjoy Cuba's numerous national parks and protected areas including

An Awesome Itinerary!

A truly awesome **Best of Cuba** trip would start with a few nights in **Havana** followed by a week at one of the beach resorts in **Cayo Coco** or **Cayo Largo**, a few nights in **Santiago**, a week fishing and scuba diving in **Los Jardines de La Reina**, a few days exploring Viñales with a day or two spent in **María La Gorda** for a little more diving. If, after all that you need to relax a little, spend 3-4 nights at **Cayo Levisa** strolling on the beach and snorkeling.

Guanahacabibes Península, Jardines de La Reina and Caguanes National Park.

Music Lovers will find the entire island alive with good music. Government support for musical education ensures top-quality musicians wherever you decide to stay. Havana and Santiago in particular have dozens of venues for live music.

If you are interested in **Cuban history and the Revolution** you will find no shortage of museums, battle sites and memorials.

4. HAVANA

HIGHLIGHTS
▲ Stroll along the famous Malecón seawall, Havana's living room

▲ Walk through Old Havana

▲ Visit Hemingway's Haunts – La Floridita and La Bodeguita del Medio

▲ Soak up music, music, music – visit the home of the Buena Vista Social Club

▲ Visit great museums & historical sites

COORDINATES

Havana, located on Cuba's northwest coast, is the capital and serves as hub for most visitors to the country. Including the UNESCO World Heritage Site, Old Havana and its Fortifications, it is one of the most fascinating cities in the world.

INTRO

Havana is one of the world's most interesting, fascinating cities throbbing with life. Crumbling, festering, sprawling, Havana is trying to make a living, refurbish and find a new way in spite of shortages of basic supplies, over regulation and long lines.

Music leaks from every window. It's hot. Few residents have air-conditioning. One of the images of Havana that sticks in my mind is the common sight of a half dozen *Habaneros* hanging out on the front porch with a deck of cards or dominoes on an old box and a bottle of rum.

Walking around **Old Havana** and strolling along the **Malecón** are a couple of the main reasons to visit Havana. Although many of the buildings suffer horribly from neglect, the government is actively renovating some of them. The charm of the Old Havana with its architecture and people is hard to describe.

Old Havana is slowly becoming a worthy tourism destination. Many of the beautiful old buildings are collapsing but others are being renovated by the government and turned into hip cafes, boutique hotels and art galleries.

HAVANA'S SIGHTS

UNESCO World Heritage Site, Old Havana and Its Fortifications is densely inhabited with everyday Cubans. Although the government is working to turn the area into a tourism destination, the neighborhoods throb with music and life.

The **Malecón** is a long concrete seawall (*see photo on previous page*) that runs all along Havana's shoreline

providing the setting for what is truly Havana's living room. There are always lots of people hanging around by the waterfront. The housing shortage means large extended families share crumbling apartments and many folks spend most of their time outdoors. It's a wonderful place for a walk almost any time of day.

EXPLORING OLD HAVANA

One of the greatest things to do in Havana is to take long walks through this **UNESCO World Heritage Site**—the Pearl of the Caribbean—Old Havana. Amazing colonial architecture, crumbling to ruins about the inhabitants, old fifties-era US cars, quaint churches and numerous tourist-oriented bars and cafes are the attractions. Watch out for water leaks dripping on to passing heads. Several interesting hotels are located here. An unbelievable 100,000 people live in this small neighborhood.

With one notable exception, there are very few places in the area I can recommend to eat but almost any bar will have loud, tourist-oriented Buena Vista Social Club-type bands cranking it out with enthusiasm. Along the waterfront, I find **El Templete** to be one of the few government-run restaurants worth sampling. I like their bar and the food is usually good. They have a decent wine list.

Old Havana is one of the best places in Cuba to wander around with a camera. The residents are quite inured to tourists and will mostly ignore you. A few famously pose for pictures for tips. Look for the old lady smoking a huge cigar.

MUSEUMS

Most of Havana's museums feature revolutionary themes. There are a couple of notable exceptions. The work of Cuba's current top artists are hard to get close to but, if you get a chance, keep an eye out for **Lazaro Niebla, Rudys Rubio, Yunieski Fernandez**, or **Esterio Segura**.

Museum of the Revolution

In the old presidential palace, the museum, *Museo de la Revolución*, like many places you will see in Cuba, is a virtual shrine to the heroes of the revolution with lots and lots of Che, Fidel and Martí photos and memorabilia. They have José Martí's bloody trousers on display. You can still see bullet holes in the stairwell from when the revolutionaries took over.

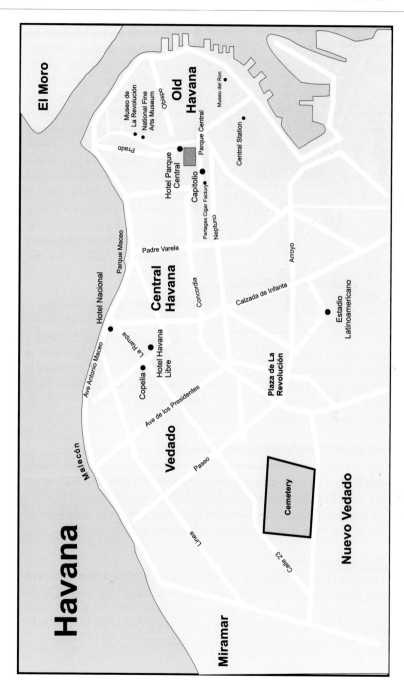

Don't forget to look upstairs on the third floor as they often have displays of local artists. This is probably something you should not miss. I know the government would like every tourist to see it and soak up their version of the events surrounding the revolution. Outside in a glass building is the *Granma*, the boat Fidel used to launch the revolution surrounded by a couple of strange old vehicle used somehow in the fighting. *Info: Calle Refugio entre Monserrate y Zulueta. Tel. 53-762-4091.*

National Fine Arts Museum

This is the big one right across the street from the old presidential palace. The large building houses some of the finest art I have seen in Cuba. The state extensively supports the arts and the result is impressively displayed here. I rate it a "don't miss" in Havana. It is by far Cuba's nicest and best run museum. *Info: Monserrate y Zulueta. CUC 8. www.museonacional.cult.cu; Tel. 537-863-9484.*

Museo del Chocolate (Chocolate Museum)

This is a café serving chocolate stuff and not really a museum even though they do have a couple of chocolate-related items in a glass case. You can get hot chocolate, chocolate milk and a few other chocolaty things but if you are serious about your chocolate don't bother. There can be quite a line to get in. The smell is great. *Info: Calle Amargura in Old Havana.*

Museo Hemingway

Formerly called the **Finca La Vigía**, Hemingway's tranquil home has been well preserved and is well worth and hour or so wandering around. There are nice views from the hilltop location. His old fishing boat the Pilar is preserved on the tennis court. You can see the graves of his favorite dogs. *Info: In the suburb of San Francisco de Paula. 3 CUC. Tel. 7-91-0809.*

Museo de la Música

The museum has a large and interesting collection of all types of musical instruments including one of the biggest collections of African drums anywhere. *Info: Calle Capdevila 1. Open 10am – 6pm every day.*

Museo del Ron

The museum spotlights **Havana Club rums** with 15-minute tours, tasting and a nice souvenir shop. The museum is in an old colonial building with a nice courtyard where you wait for your tour to start. Tours are in English, Spanish, French and German. The guides explain the entire process of making rum from growing the sugar cane to aging. The nice Havana Club Bar is next door if you want to continue your exploration of rum after the tour. *Info: Avenida del Puerto 262.*

HAVANA BUS TOUR

For a good overview of the city it is hard to beat the hop on and hop off double-decker bus tour. There is not much spoken commentary but enough to get you oriented. There are three routes that cover the city from touristic end to touristic end. You can get off and back on at over 60 stops for a mere CUC 5. Yes it is touristy but we are, after all, tourists and this is by far the best way to become familiar with the city for a nominal cost. The tours run from 9am to 9pm every day. Look for them on the west side of Parque Central. *Info: CUC 5 per day. www.transtur.cu; Tel. 537-835-000.*

PARTAGAS CIGAR FACTORY

Packed with tour groups the **cigar factory** is probably the best place to see the whole cigar making routine. Guides explain the growing, selection and rolling processes. The guide I was with spoke excellent English. You get to see the actual workers cranking out big cigars. The shop has all the best ones. You have to buy a ticket at one of the hotels—you can't just walk up and buy a ticket at the door. You are not allowed to take photographs. The cigars in the shop are high-priced—you can do better elsewhere. *Info: CUC 10. Calle Industrial 520.*

NECROPOLIS CRISTOBAL COLON -
BEST OFF-THE-BEATEN PATH SIGHTSEEING

The **Havana cemetery** is definitely a sight to see. The crypts, tombs, statuary and headstones are elaborate—some nicer and large than houses. You will see signs of Santaria worship. Admission is $5 CUC and an

Copelia

Havana boasts one the world's most interesting **ice cream emporiums**. The huge flying-saucer-shaped **Copelia** building in Vedado at the top of La Rampa can seat hundreds of ice cream lovers at the same time. Flavors change daily but the quality is always high. It costs just pennies for an *ensalada*—a bowl of 4 different scoops with chocolate sauce. *¡Delicioso!*

excellent guidebook + site map is available for $1 CUC. It is located a short walking distance from Casa Antigua, on Calzada de Zapata at Calle 12. The cab drivers all know it.

HAVANA'S FOUR SECTIONS

There are four distinct parts of the rambling city that are of interest to visitors. If you have more than a week to enjoy the city, you may decide to stay in the quaint **Old Havana** for a couple of nights to enjoy the nearby sights and then spend a few nights in **Miramar** or **Vedado**. Near the Parque Central in **El Centro**, for the maximum comfort and a fairly central location, **Hotel Parque Central** is hard to beat.

El Centro includes the area around the **Parque Central, Capitolio** and east past the huge **Hospital Hermanos Ameijeiras**. This used to be one of the main shopping districts but is now mostly crumbling residential buildings in need of restoration. A couple of good paladars are located in this area. **Vedado** used to be Havana's commercial center and still is home to airline offices and tour agencies. Some of the city's best music venues are here. The **University of Havana** is well worth a stroll. I suggest walking through the lobby of the **Tryp Havana Libre** (used to be the Hilton) to see a prime example of kitschy US 1950's interior design.

For sure have a drink on the patio at the **Hotel Nacional** (*see photo below*) and soak up some of the Meyer Lanksy mystique. With luck the hotel will

be hosting a *quincenaria*, a young lady's 15th birthday celebration. Check out the classic 1950s American cars parked out front.

RUSSIAN EMBASSY

The enormous city block-size **Russian Embassy** is worth a look, but don't

linger trying to count the many antennas on the roof. It's not usually a tourist site.

BASEBALL

If you are a sports fan Havana has two major league stadiums and, in season, there are several **baseball** games every week. Cuba boasts

18 national-level teams organized in two leagues. The country is famous for producing such baseball greats as **Rolando Arrojo, Jose Contreras**, and **Dayan Vicideo**. The quality of play in local stadiums is extremely high.

Baseball season runs from November to May with the playoffs usually scheduled for June. There are two stadiums in Havana which are large and reasonably well equipped but may seem primitive to US fans. The quality of play is far, far from primitive. Take a taxi to the game and arrange for the driver to meet you when the game is over. Both stadiums are a long walk from the central area. Check at www.baseballdecuba.com for game schedules and more information.

Museums, paladars, music venues and places of touristic interest are often far apart and you will probably find yourself using taxis to get around. Still, Havana is a great walking town and you will probably stretch your legs quite a bit. If you walk through the **Parque Central** you will usually see a small crowd of baseball fanatics gesticulating and talking loud on the **east side of the park near the fountain**. These guys gather everyday to discuss the sport of el *beisbol* in great detail. Join in if your Spanish is up to it.

For more information, see page 59.

BEST SLEEPS & EATS
Sleeps

Havana is poor, poor, poor, but it can be extremely expensive for a visitor. The few decent hotels charge top international rates even though they are simply not up to international standards in many respects. Some high-priced hotels can be almost uninhabitable.

There are a couple of very good hotels in Havana. Some feature more "character" than international-standards luxury. Book early as the best ones tend to fill up quickly.

There are also a plethora of **truly horrible lodging** choices. Some of the grand old hotels are in sad need of renovating and should probably be closed. Understand that even the best hotels sometimes show their guests unpleasant experiences—no towels, grimy sheets, dysfunctional plumbing, not hot water, too much hot water, surly service, the list goes on and on. Choose carefully and be prepared to make minor compromises.

Casas Particulares, private homes specially licensed by the government to rent rooms to tourists, are a popular and economical choice in a town where hotels are notoriously overpriced. Be aware that unless they have a license from the government, it is against the law for Cuban citizens to let foreigners stay in their homes overnight. Vigilant neighborhood watch-type organizations enforce this law fairly strictly.

EL CENTRO
There are several nice lodging choices around and nearby the Central Park area, notably the conveniently named **Hotel Parque Central**. It is a large, comfortable, modern, international hotel with a new section approaching five star status. The restaurants are good for Cuba but still leave much lacking.

BEST OF THE BEST IN HAVANA –
THE AUTHOR'S FAVORITE HOTEL IN CUBA
Parque Central $$$$$
Still fairly new, in good condition, and by far the best hotel in the entire country, the Parque flirts with being an international-quality

businessman's hotel. The location, right on the Central Park, is superb. The huge lobby has a great bar, Wi-Fi and is the scene of a tide of international tourists and business types seeking

---

the comfort they are used to when traveling internationally—something not easy to find in Cuba. The newer section next door is slightly nicer and flirts with elegance.

The rooms are large, well appointed with good mattresses and good linen. The breakfast buffet is typically Cuban: plenty of bread and pastries, eggs, meatballs and somehow, never quite enough fruit. Most service in the hotel is also typically Cuban: indifferent. Still, this is an excellent hotel by any standards. *Info: Neptuno el Prado y Zultueta Habana. www.hotelparquecentral.com; Tel. 537-860-6627.*

Inglaterra $$$

The glory of the past is evident in the grand old lady of the Inglaterra but, unfortunately, the beauty has pretty much faded—little more than the wrinkles remain. It is certainly worthwhile to have a drink on the patio in front and walk through the lobby to gaze up at the detail in tile, plaster and discolored gilt. But don't stay there. The rooms are small, stink and most seem to have several amenities that simply are broken—like faucets.

Because of its location right on the square, traffic noises echo around inside bouncing off the concrete walls, ceilings and marble floors. The rooms are gloomy and, I think I already said this, run-down. For over $100 for a double it is just not worth it, in fact, I find the place to be almost uninhabitable. *Info: Paseo del Prado, No. 416 esq. San Rafael. www.hotelinglaterra-cuba.com; Tel. 07- 864-9177.*

Hurricanes?

Hurricane season officially lasts from **June 1 to November 30** but hurricanes can come as late as December. From time to time tourists may be asked to evacuate as approaching storms threaten. Monitor weather reports before and during your trip to Cuba during hurricane season.

Hotel Plaza $$$

A classic beauty right on the corner of the park, the Plaza has retained some of its historical charm. The rooms are large, dark and, I found, most of the amenities sort-of work. The last time I stayed, I had plenty of scalding hot water in the shower but, strangely, no cold water. The closet doorknob fell off in my hand every time I used it.

The lobby bar is nice but loud. The location at the edge of the park and the edge of old Havana is ideal. The interior is an architectural wonder. Babe Ruth stayed here once and Albert Einstein spent two hours here once, for some reason. The staff can seem indifferent but, if you have problems, just wait a few minutes and find another staff member to help you. They seem to have hundreds of people "working" there. *Info: Calle Ignacio Agramonte No. 267, Habana Vieja. www.hotelplazacuba.com; Tel. 537- 860-8583.*

Hotel Saratoga $$$$

Recently renovated, the hotel has comfortable beds and is nicely located near the Capitolio and Old Havana. The rooftop pool is attractive but you probably will not choose to swim since it always seems to need cleaning. The food is okay at breakfast but for other meals, very expensive and very mediocre.

Views from most rooms are good, looking out over Havana rooftops from the higher floors. Of course their five star rating is absurd. Like most Cuban hotels, it is not quite up to the standard they claim. The Parque Central is nearby and is much nicer. Overall, it is a disappointment for the money. *Info: Avenida Paseo del Prado. www.saratogahotel-cuba.com; Tel. 7- 868-1000.*

Casa Antigua $

Horacio & Marta, offer two rooms with a shared bath. Horacio, himself a pianist, knows where the nightlife and music is happening in town. Breakfast is good and features the man himself on piano. It is up a flight of stairs in a particularly fine old mansion. The location is fairly central. *Info: Vedado, Calle 28, # 258 entre 21 y 23.*

Casa Évora $

Casa Évora is on the 9th floor of an old embassy building at the bottom end of Paseo del Prado with an incredible view over Havana and the Malecón and popular Castillo del Morro. Laundry is included in the price! Let's not talk about the elevator. Evora speaks good English and is famous for her pancakes. This is my favorite place to stay in Havana and, since many other people feel the same way, it is hard to book. *Info: Paeso del Prado No 20.*

OLD HAVANA

Right in the middle of Havana's most charming neighborhood, **Old Havana** has some recently created boutique hotels that are loaded with character and are reasonably comfortable.

Hostal Los Frailes $$$

The quaint monastery has been turned into a 22-room boutique hotel. The theme is rather gimmicky with the staff wearing heavy brown robes in the Havana heat. Some rooms have windows. It is nice overall and fairly quiet in a touristy part of the Old Havana. It is one of the nicer hotel renovations that have been happening in the last couple of years in this part of town. They have an intimate lobby bar. Breakfast is across the street to a restaurant but it is not up to the same standards as the hotel. Walking tours of the Old Havana sometimes intrude into the public areas. *Info: Calle Teniente Rey No. 8 el Mercaderes y Oficios. www.hotellosfrailescuba.com; Tel. 7-864-9177.*

Casa 1932 $

This casa particular is on a dodgy-looking street, has some nice antiques, private bathroom with hot water, room safe, helpful family, nice location only a block from the Malecón. Breakfast and dinners are good. Louis Miguel is a great host and will do an airport pickup. With only two rooms it is difficult to book. *Info: Campanario No 63 (Bajos) | el San Lazaro y Lagunas.*

Casa Dania $

Located in the heart of Old Havana, hosts Dania and Giovanni (not much English) serve good food on their outdoor terrace. They have one double and one triple both with nice private bathrooms. It is up three flights of stairs. Charlie, a nice pooch, has free run of the place. *Info: Calle Obrapia No.460, Apt:5 entre Villegas y Aguacate.*

VEDADO

Vedado, once Havana's business center, is now where much of the city's best music venues are located. It has a couple of very interesting lodging choices, particularly the **Nacional** and the **Havana Try-Libre**.

Nacional $$$

Built in 1931 by notorious mobster Meyer Lansky, the Nacional is loaded with character. The tiled Moroccan-style lobby is a remarkable sight. This is one of my favorites with great views of the Malecón and Havana skyline from some of the higher rooms.

The rooms are only slightly run-down and have most of the modern hotel amenities you would expect: hair dryers, mini-bar, in-room safe (but they charge you extra to use them), phones and TV with international stations. If you can get a room with a view of Havana Bay you have done well—they have wonderful views out to sea.

The breakfast buffet is mid-quality with a wide variety of pastries, eggs, undercooked bacon and a meager selection of canned fruit. The fresh-squeezed orange juice is superb. The restaurant coffee is terrible but you can buy a good cup in the lobby bar for only $2.50. I avoid all the restaurants but a beer on the back patio can be relaxing. I like the place.

The hotel has been maintained since the revolution primarily with lots of caulk and thick coats of paint. Original Buena Vista Social Club member Compay Segundo entertains on weekends. *Info: Vedado, Calle 21 y O. www.hotelnacionaldecuba.com; Tel. 7-836-3564.*

Havana Libre Tryp $$$

Back in the old days this was the Hilton and there is still an "H" on the bottom of the pool. The casino was mob run and, when the revolutionaries swept into town, they set themselves up here and booted out all the gringo leeches.

The rooms are large and reasonably comfortable although the mattresses need replacing a little more frequently. Views out to sea from the upper floor, ocean-facing rooms are superb. The lobby is loud, busy and features the personality of a bus station. It is located in Varadero a long walk away from Old Havana. *Info: Calle L entre 23 y 25. Tel. 7-834-6100.*

MIRAMAR

Miramar, one of Havana's premier residential areas, houses many embassies and corporate headquarters buildings in grand old homes built during the big money mobster era. Some of the best Paladars are located there.

Panorama Hotel $$$

The Panorama has great views, it's fairly new, nice, with a large pool, terrible food and service as usual. It is a modern high-rise with atrium and cool, glass-fronted elevators. Not a very good location, though. In Miramar, it is at least within walking distance of a couple of nice paladars but you will need a taxi to go almost anywhere. *Info: Playa, 3rd Ave and 70th St.*

Occidental Miramar $$$

This place was brand new when I stayed and but already had plenty of rough edges and some things were already broken. The food was some of the worst I have encountered in any Cuban hotel. Carpets in the corridors did not quite fit and it seems they had cannibalized many of the rooms in order to provide at least a few rooms that have all the necessary pieces. It is located at the far end of Miramar and, unless you find the Russian embassy interesting, there is almost nothing in the area of interest

Credit Card Issues

I am always careful to call my credit card companies before any overseas trip alerting them to my plans to use their cards in some strange place, like Cuba. They always thank me for telling them and assure me they have made a note of it in the computer and that there will be no problems. In spite of this they almost always block my cards as soon as they realize someone is trying to use them in such an outlandish place and I have to call them a second time (expensively) to get them to unblock the cards.

to visitors. My advice: skip it. *Info: Miramar, 5ᵗʰ Ave entre 72 y 76. Tel. 7-204-3449.*

Meliá Cohiba $$$

Not centrally located but the walk into Old Havana is pleasant. They also have a free minibus that runs from time to time. They are right across from the Malecón in Vedado. The very typical breakfast buffet is a little on the skimpy side. The coffee is terrible but they will bring you an espresso for no extra charge if you ask. There is an adequate Italian restaurant . There is a concierge desk and a pool. Some rooms have a nice view of the ocean. You can watch freighters coming in to Havana harbor while soaking in your tub. Poolside food is overpriced and lame. The attached night spot the Havana Club is a bit seedy as are some of its denizens. Breakfast buffet is on the 20ᵗʰ floor with great views. *Info: Ave. Paseo entre 1ᵃ y 3ᵃ. www.solmelia.com; Tel. 7-833-3636 or from US 888-95-MELIA.*

Casa Habana Lourdes $

Lourdes and her family prepare good meals and offer good travel advice. Marvel, Lourdes's daughter, speaks English. Located only a couple of blocks from the Capitolio, the building is vaguely Gaudiesque—intriguing. The rooms are quiet and private. The bath, shared with the other room, is across the hall and offers a suicide shower (electric showerhead heats the water). *Info: Teniente Rey (Brasil) 361 e/ Aguacate y Villegas.*

Eats

It is a big mistake to expect Havana or Cuba in general to be an interesting culinary destination. My friends in the states think Cuban food is wonderful, spicy and exotic. That may be the case in Miami but *not* in Cuba. Because there is little incentive to grow vegetables and fruit, both are in short supply. Even limes can be scarce. Salt and pepper rarely appear on dining tables. Hot peppers? Hot sauce? Forget about it. Cuban food is invariable bland—even in the privately run paladars.

Almost without exception, any eatery run by the government has dire food—sometimes to the point of inedibility. This includes all the hotels, restaurants and snack bars. **Paladars**, privately run but highly regulated restaurants in peoples' homes, can be wonderful exceptions. Long oases of good food, they have gotten better and better and, due to the government's recent liberalizing of laws controlling them, there are more of paladars than ever. **La Guarida**, where much of the movie *Fresa y Chocolate* was filmed, is one of the most illustrious and best. The memorable **Cocina de Lilliam** where a small goldfish bowl sometimes appears on a plate is a great and romantic dining experience.

When choosing a paladar for dinner, it is a good idea to call ahead to see if they still exist. The more popular ones fill up rapidly in the evenings but will take reservations. Taxi drivers will often insist that your dining choice is closed and take you to a government-run place instead where they can get a referral fee. Insist on going to your choice and get out of the cab if the driver is being difficult. This happens a lot. Some drivers will simply take you to another place and insist it is the one you asked for.

Havana is a large city and restaurants can be an expensive taxi ride from your hotel.

Miramar is host to embassies, discrete corporate headquarters and homes to some upscale government officials. A couple of Havana's best paladars are located here. **Vista Mar** and **Cocina de Lilliam** offer elegant, romantic and delicious dining.

EL CENTRO
La Guarida $$$
Recently reopened after a battle with government regulators, in an old, elegant house in a not so nice neighborhood, this *paladar* is one of the best in town and is quite popular. Reservations are a good idea unless you arrive early (6pm or so). The interesting menu includes things like rabbit lasagna and several fish dishes. They have a full bar and crank out great frozen daiquiris. Okay Chilean wines by the glass are $3. The doorman will get you a cab when it's time to go. The movie *Chocolate y Fresa* starring Vladimir Cruz and Jorge Perugorría was partially filmed there. *Info: Centro Habana, Calle Concordia #418 e/ Gervasio y Escobar. www.laguarida.com/en; Tel. 7-862-4940.*

Hotel Nacional $$$

There are several restaurants in the hotel, none worth going out of your way for. The opposite may be true. The hotel's included breakfast has a good selection of fresh, dried and canned fruit, a buffet of undercooked bacon and eggs, and the usual omelet station with the omelets already made and going cold. They have great fresh squeezed orange juice. The basement cafeteria is not really a cafeteria and offers sullen service and stale food. Skip it.

Their upscale restaurant, **Comedor de Aguilar**, claims to be carefully preserving Meyer Lansky's original 1930s atmosphere. They do a good job of that but it seems much of the food may be left over from that era as well. It is *waaay* overpriced for what is on offer. *Info: Vedado, Calle 21 y O. www.hotelnacionaldecuba.com; Tel. 7-836-3564.*

OLD HAVANA
El Templete $$$

At El Templete, the walls are covered with wonderful art—some of it hanging on the walls and some of it painted directly on the walls. I love the bar. It is one of the few bars in town where they pour without benefit of measuring in a shot glass. The food is consistently good, unusual in a government-run restaurant. The location near the waterfront offers good people watching if you sit in the outdoor patio. The pargo (snapper) is wonderful. Service is fine and the wine list is extensive. There are usually lots of foreign business types enjoying the interesting menu selections. *Info: Ave. del Puerto esq. Narciso López. Tel. 7-866-8807.*

VEDADO
Paladar Nieto $$

On the corner, only one block from Copelia, Nieto offers a reasonable selection of steak, chicken and fish dishes accompanied by the usual rice and beans and fried plantains. The service is reasonably good and the food better prepared than most of the government-run places but there are much better choices nearby. Check your bill against the menu before you pay. *Info: Calle 19 y Calle L.*

Coppelia $

You simply must visit Cuba's famous ice cream emporium at least once. Located in the middle of the park at the top of La Rampa, it is extremely popular with Cubans—you will almost certainly have to wait in line a half hour or more to get in, but it's worth it. They have several serving areas and it is a good idea to stroll around a little before deciding which area you would like for your ice cream adventure.

People are usually seated together in small groups. Waitresses take orders from everyone and bring out the goodies for all at the same time. You can also buy some frozen Coppelia goodies from kiosks around the perimeter of the park. This stuff from the kiosks outside is good, but not as good as the ice cream delights you get when you wait in line and sit down inside.

When you approach the place you will see the lines but it is often difficult to figure out where the end of the line is. Simply ask: *el ultimo?* The end? And someone will tell you who the last one in line is. Cubans are used to waiting in lines and are quite civilized about it. No queue jumpers here! Often, people waiting in line will actually be sitting on a nearby wall or chatting with their pals a few yards away. This is cool. When the line moves, everyone knows whose place in line is whose. No pena. *Info: Calle L y La Rampa.*

MIRAMAR
Il Diluvio $$
This delightful Italian paladar run by the outgoing Walter, features octopus salad, focaccia with fresh fish, pasta and other Italian-inspired delights. It is not particularly fancy but the atmosphere is great. The whole family seems to be waiting on you (including the dog) and all spend the evening laughing, smiling, joking (pouring ice down the ladies' fronts and indulging in general horseplay. They have a wood-burning pizza oven! I love the place. I suggest letting Walter make all the selections for you. No matter what I eat, two glasses of wine and dinner always seems to cost me $CUC 25. Not bad for all you get. It is in Miramar in a residential neighborhood. *Info: Playa. Calle 72, entre 17 y 19. Tel. 53-202-1531.*

American Chow

Pizza and spaghetti are very common in Cuba. Hamburgers are usually dire since beef is at a premium and is rarely grain fed. A cheeseburger by the pool will probably be a disappointment. There are really no fast food chains at all.

Vistamar $$$$

Vista Mar, one of the best places to eat in Havana, is an upscale eatery favored by young moneyed Cubans. Lobster, shrimp, crab—all the top goodies are on offer. They have a nice downstairs bar you can hang in while waiting for your table. Try to reserve ahead to get one of the tables on the balcony overlooking the sea. You'll see high government officials, businessmen and diplomats showing off their beautiful Cuban girlfriends. The food is wonderful and presented on square plates with colorful drizzly sauces and garnished with herb sprigs. Very nice. *Info: Avenida 1 entre Calle 22 y 23 . Tel. 7-203-8328.*

BEST OF THE BEST IN HAVANA –
THE AUTHOR'S FAVORITE RESTAURANT IN CUBA
La Cocina de Lilliam $$$

This is one of the greatest places to eat on the island. The simple paladar has tables set in a lovely garden. A classical guitarist accompanies diners. Very romantic. For a nice night out with your sweetie, this is hard to beat. The last time I visited, I had a simple grilled mahi with a wonderful vegetable salad. Included on my plate was a small fish bowl with an actual goldfish swimming around in it. Really! I told the waiter I didn't like sushi. He didn't seem to get the joke. Reservations are a good idea. *Info: Calle 48 No. 1311 e/13 y 15. Playa. Tel. 537-209-6514. 12pm-3pm, 7pm-10pm, Closed Sundays.*

El Gringo Viejo $$$
This is a very nice basement paladar decorated as a shrine to Anthony Quinn and his movie Last Train to Yuma, perhaps the most popular US movie in Cuba. The food runs to seafood and pasta. It takes a few minutes to get through their security but it is well worth it. Upper class Cubans, foreigners working for NGOs and a few tourists are the main customers. *Info: Calle 21 # 454. Tel. 7-831-1946.*

Cuban Coffee

Cuba is famous for its strong, hot brew. Cubans usually enjoy it black in tiny cups with three or more spoons of sugar. Cuban coffee is not for the faint of heart but you can usually get the thin, weak *café Americano* if you ask. *Café con leche* usually comes with hot milk. Wonderful! **Cubita** is the best brand to buy to take back home.

Typical Cuban Dishes

Moros y Cristianos – rice and black beans
Ropa Vieja – sautéed strips of flank steak
Puerco Asado – pulled pork
Caldo Gallego – a stew made of ham, pork chunks, chorizo sausage and white beans

BEST SHOPPING

Shopping is poor but Che t-shirts are plentiful. Shopping is not a reason to visit Cuba but Havana does have a few things worth bringing home. The main items on sale to tourists are Che t-shirts, Elian t-shirts, and more Che t-shirts.

Located on the harbor near where cruise ships might dock, Havana's **Craft & Souvenir** market has a better selection of things you might want to take home for gifts or souvenirs than any place else on the island. The sterile building houses dozens of identical stalls selling paintings, jewelry, t-shirts, hats and some leatherwork. It is closed on Mondays and Tuesdays.

BEST NIGHTLIFE & ENTERTAINMENT

There is seriously a lot to do in Havana. There are dozens, if not hundreds of musical, dance and theater performances *every day*. Nightlife is world famous. There are dozens of historic and cool bars with live music playing almost every day.

Nightlife in Havana is HOT! HOT! HOT! ¡*Candela!* No matter what time it is, there is something going on. It's a late night town with many musical acts not beginning until after midnight. If you happen to drive along the

Malecón at 5am or 6am on almost any morning you will see large crowds of leftover partiers carrying things on just a little bit longer.

Cuba's is justly world-famous for its **music** scene. It seems like every corner bar and café has a live combo at lunch and a loud salsa band at night. There are dozens of bars, nightclubs, and concert venues hosting bands of all types every night. Many hotels feature *espectáculos* and elaborate stage shows. Intimate jazz clubs and hot discos open late, late and close around dawn.

WATERING HOLES
There are dozens of corner bars, cafes and hotel bars to have a drink or two in and soak up the atmosphere and watch the passing parade. Some of the more famous ones are crowded with tourists but, if you are a tourist, no big deal. Just crowd right on in there with the rest of us.

El Floridita
On the corner of Obispo y Monserrate, the Floridita is home to the delicious **daiquiri** even if, sadly, it is made better almost anywhere else. Hemingway, Errol Flynn and other cool dudes used the bar as one of their main hangouts and their spirits linger. The drinks are not so hot and the place is always jammed with tourists. At night, they have a very cool blue neon sign out front.

Bodeguita del Medio
This is yet another of Hemingway's old haunts. There is a small bar up front and a large dining area in the back. It has been completely remodeled several times since the Old Man hung out but it is still worth a visit. Mojitos are the deal here.

Bar at the Hotel Nacional
Overlooking the sea and the Malecón, the Hotel Nacional has a great terrace bar in the back garden. The seating is very comfortable and the drinks cold. I like to hang here from time to time listening to the strolling combo. You can also go inside and sit in the air-conditioned lobby.

LIVE MUSIC VENUES
In Old Havana almost every bar and café has a live band cranking it out for the tourists. Although aimed at tourists, the music is almost always great. Cuba's musicians are *all* well trained and *all* good or they wouldn't be allowed out in front of people.

Like in any big city, it can be a little difficult to figure out who's playing where and what the great bands are. Having a friend who is aware helps but, if you don't know anyone who can clue you in, try this web site: *www.canalcubano.com/ingles/musica/musica.asp*.

For late night music, **La Zorra y El Cuervo** on La Rampa is one of the most popular spots for Latin jazz. **Cine Yara** at the top of La Rampa often hosts major bands such as Los Van Van and Chucho Valdez. The **Jazz Café** and **El Gato Tuerto** are also famous nightlife choices.

Pot? Drugs?

Due to its location halfway between the drug sources in South America and the consumers in the US, Cuba has a growing drug situation. Unfortunately the police presence is uncooperative with a doper lifestyle. They are very serious about busting anyone using any type of illegal drugs and there are *many* informers lurking about. The airports have many drug dogs sniffing about. Skip Cuba if you are a serious pothead.

World-famous artists like **Los Van Van** and **Chucho Valdez** play in Havana from time to time. A couple of remaining members of the **Buena Vista Social Club** play at the Hotel Nacional. **Compay Segundo** is there several times a week. But realize that dozens and dozens of performers *claim* some connection with the famous group.

Some of the best bands to catch: Los Van Van, Manolito Simonet Y Su Trabuco, La Charanga Habanera, Bamboleo, and Havana d'Primera. One of the best things about the Havana music scene is the matinees. Several of the large clubs offer the same big names they have in the evenings in the afternoons around 5pm for about half the price.

One of the bad things about the Havana music scene is the excruciating wait for the main act to start in the evenings. The headliners tend to start very, very, very late—sometimes after 2am with several hours of over loud reggaeton to be endured beforehand. Dreadful comedians, magicians and tumbling acts can also affront the music lover. Bear with it. Cubans seem to love an *espectáculo*, a long show with dozens of novelty acts, and like to spend hours dancing to music videos and DJs who have been watching too much MTV before the main act comes on. The locals are out for the whole night—not just to see the headliner.

Radio station Canal Cubano keeps a good listing of who's playing where on their web site: *www.canalcubano.com/ ingles/musica/musica.asp*.

Gato Tuerto
A trendy, happening, intimate jazz club with top quality local artists, the "**One-Eyed-Cat**" caters to a slightly older crowd—this is not a salsa club. Some of the older styles can be heard here including the still-popular jazz style known as "**Feelin.**'" There is little point in showing up much before midnight unless you just want to try to get a table near the stage (not necessarily a good idea). Every act I have seen here has been top quality. Drinks are good but, as is so common in Cuba's clubs and bars, service is slow and surly and the waitresses conniving. Check your bill and change very carefully. They don't seem to be worried about tips. They have other ways of getting your dollars. I like to think I am good at not being ripped off in places like this, but they manage to snatch a few extra dollars from me every time I go. I keep going though. *Info: Calle 0, e/ 17 y 19, Vedado, Habana. Tel. 537-836-0212.*

Casa de La Música
The two locations, one in central Havana and one in Miramar are famous for their large, spectacular stage shows with dancing girls and huge salsa bands. Both places open at 11pm but there is no point at all in getting there before 1am unless you like dancing to lousy music videos. Locals seem to love the place and I have met tourists who swear it is great but I find it to be a cheesy bore. It just takes forever for the music to get going and the bands, although elaborately staged, seem waaay too self impressed. Whoever sets the shows up has been watching far too many MTV-like music videos.

Both locations are usually crawling with sexy young Cuban girls, some accompanied by older gringos. Most tourists seem to get tired and leave before the live music even starts. You may like it. I would not bother going unless I am sure a band I like, such as Los Van Van, is headlining. *Info: 155 Avenida de Italia, CUC 25; Tel. 537-860-8297. Calle 20 Miramar. CUC 20, Tel. 537-202-6147.*

Jazz Cafe

A real Havana classic, the Jazz Café has hosted all the greats, Chucho Valdez, Ornette Coleman, James Brown and many others. It is a reliable good night out. The music will be top notch. Most evenings feature a relatively short set of rhythmic Latin jazz with horns and seemingly dozens of drums and varied percussion instruments. The only problem I have with the place is nothing starts happening until at least midnight. There is a $10 minimum but the prices are reasonable—I rarely drink up my minimum. It is comfortable with good service. *Info: Calle Paseo y 3ra., Vedado. Tel. 537-838-3302.*

La Zorra y El Cuervo (The Fox and the Crow)

This is basement club is one of the best places in Havana for live music. Most featured groups are jazz bands. Doors usually open at 11pm and the music starts up about midnight. There is a CUC 5 cover. Well worth it every time I have been. *Info: Calle 23 y O, La Rampa, Vedado. Tel. 537-833-2402.*

Salon Rosado Benny More

This open-air venue is about as *auténtico* as it gets. It is one of the top places—all the famous bands have played here. Shows are almost always packed with a 100% Cuban audience. Sunday afternoons are devoted to more traditional style of son with dancing slightly more restrained than the *casino* style of dance that accompanies more recent styles of *timba*. Foreigners are usually directed to the upstairs patio where drinks are more expensive and the air slightly more refined. I love the place but it's a pretty involved night out. You will almost certainly be the only gringo there. *Info: Playa, Avenida 41 y 46. Tel. 29-0985, 23-5322.*

SHOWS

Cuba is famous for elaborate stage shows involving dancing girls in complicated, skimpy outfits with lots of feathers, glitter and legs. The most famous of these places is, without a

Prostitution

Cuba, and Havana in particular, has earned a reputation for casual prostitution aimed at foreigners. Pretty young ladies wearing nice dresses lurk in front of many nightclubs and music venues hoping to catch the eye of a visiting gringo. Most are hoping for a night out—drinks, food, dancing—and maybe more. The government reaction to this free enterprise varies. From time to time there are roundups and the ladies are sent to the fields to pick oranges or sugar cane for a couple of months of "reeducation."

doubt, the **Tropicana**. **Casa de La Música** (*see above under music venues*) with two locations and featuring hours and hours of synchronized dancing, crazy costumes and eventually, usually beginning about 3am in the morning, good headline music acts.

It's a bit much for me but many tourists swear it is one of their best experiences in Cuba. Most of the shows have the exotic dancing girls followed by a long procession of jugglers, magicians, acrobats, fire-eaters, and such. These shows are called *espectáculos* (spectacles) and indeed they are. Cubans love this stuff. I can't stand it.

Tropicana $$$$

The Tropicana casino was so successful during the 1950s, they raffled off a brand new Buick convertible every Saturday afternoon to day-trippers flying in from Miami for the slots, girls and booze. The gambling and much of the ambiance is gone but the booze and beautiful girls remain. I suppose this cabaret is a "do not miss" Havana experience but some visitors say they feel like cattle being herded in and out after their wallets have been lightened as much as possible.

The show is what is called an "espectáculo" or spectacle and includes a bottle of rum and four cokes per table. Some tables have a much better view than others. Package tours that include the show often put their customers in sections of tables far to the side or even in back where the show is just not visible. Be sure to check on where your seats will be before confirming. Eat before you go as the food and service are terrible. Beer goes for CUC 5 and poor-quality wine for an incredible CUC 35.

They want CUC 5 for you to take photographs. Just understand this is not a *Cuban* experience. It is a *tourist* experience. "Overpriced tourist trap" is a comment I have heard several times. *Info: CUC 125. Calle 72 el 41 y 45, Mariano, Havana. Tel. 537-267-1717.*

DANCING
Club Salseando Chevere
This is the place to go in Havana if you want to salsa dance. The club's salsa show team, the "Danza Chevere," is a great dance group that makes everyone get involved in the dancing—even if you've never danced salsa before. They take you by the hand and help you dance the salsa night away! *Info*: *Calle 49C y 28 A, Reparto Kohly. Tel. 535-264-9692.*

BEST SPORTS & RECREATION

BASEBALL
Baseball (*el beisbol*) is absolutely wonderful in Cuba. A visit to one of the two stadiums in Havana for an afternoon or evening game, *un partido*, is well worth the US$0.05 entry fee. The stadiums are basic with concrete seats. The fans are amazing. The players are extremely good. There are no hot dog vendors and no place to buy ball caps or souvenirs. You can usually buy the traditional spam sandwiches. Try to have a few cents worth of *moneda nacional* CUPs (not CUCs) to buy a drink.

Ask at the front desk of your hotel about games. I am always surprised by how much almost anyone I ask knows about baseball. It is very popular. Most games are in the afternoon but some take place at night. It can be almost impossible to get a taxi after the game. Cubans rarely use taxis and few tourists go to the games so taxis have no reason to wait around.

Cuban players are regularly poached by US teams. Many of the very best players in the US were trained in Cuba. Even though the teams are of a world class the facilities can seem bare bones. Money is obviously tight: when balls are hit into the stands, small boys run to get them and then, reluctantly throw them back onto the field. Balls are too hard to come by to let the fans take them home. *Info: www.baseballdecuba.com.*

GOLF
There is a reasonable 9-holer golf course on the outskirts of Havana. **Club de Golf Habana**, *Carretera de Vento, Boyeros, Tel. 7-204-5700*, also has five tennis courts and a pool.

FISHING
Marina Hemingway, just west of Havana, is famous as a base for offshore fishing for marlin, sailfish and other large game fish. The Gulf Stream is close to shore along the north coast of Cuba although the very best fishing

of this type is found much further to the west. Unfortunately there are almost no facilities in those areas. If you want to go for billfish, this is really your only option.

As in many tourist destinations, I find that most of the charters available through the hotels and booking agents are simply slow, expensive boat rides— the captains don't really seem to care if you catch anything or not. The best fishing in Cuba is for smaller game fish: bonefish, tarpon, permit, grouper and kingfish, off the southwest coast of the island. **Avalon** books fishing trips to Los Jardines de La Reina, Cayo Largo and Isla de La Juventud. *Info: cubanfishingcenters.com.*

That fisherman above is me, by the way, about to release a small tarpon.

Marlin SA
Fishing charters are run out of Marina Hemingway on the western outskirts of town. The Gulf Stream is not far offshore so the fishing can be very good but captains can also be very unenthusiastic. They get CUC 375 for all day. *Info: Marina Hemingway, Canal B. Tel. 7-204-1150.*

BEACHES, PARKS & ECO-WALKS
The best seaside walk is the **Malecón**, the road that runs along the coast in front of Havana. With a concrete seawall and a couple of miles of sidewalk, it is a good opportunity to see Cubans at play and admire the crumbling architecture of what once were and are slowly becoming again, wonderful homes and offices dating from the forties and fifties. At times, waves crash over the seawall completely soaking the street, pedestrians and traffic. At night, the Malecón is hugely busy with mostly young Cubans out for a stroll for socializing, meeting new or old lovers, playing music, drinking rum from the bottle and fishing. Bring your camera.

I am told that the area of the Malecón just below the Hotel Nacional is the gay hang out. The crowds there are huge—by far the largest along the walkway. It is always packed at night. Several times when I had cause to be up at 4am or later and passed by, I saw hundreds and hundreds of partiers still there doing their thing. What a scene!

If you have time, a trip to Havana's **Playas del Este** is an interesting day out (*see photo below*). Popular with Cubans, this is a chance to see the locals at play. The beach is not one of Cuba's finest, by far, but certainly worth a visit. It's clean with nice white sand. You can buy refreshments at the few kiosks near the road and there are some decent restaurants for fish and lobster. Keep an eye on your valuables.

5. VARADERO

HIGHLIGHTS
▲ Enjoy Varadero's famous white sand beaches

▲ Sample resort nightlife with elaborate stage shows

▲ Although limited, shopping in Varadero is better than in most other resort areas

▲ Water sports!!! Kayaking, sailing, wave runners, scuba, fishing, catamarans

COORDINATES

Varadero is a long, narrow peninsula about two hours east of Havana. Most of the nicer resorts are at the eastern end. There is a small community with some stores and clubs. The beaches are some of the best in Cuba.

INTRO

Varadero was Cuba's first all-inclusive beach destination and possibly still the premier, most popular resort area in the country. There are dozens of resort choices in all price ranges and some things to do outside of the resorts. Most visitors stay for about a week coming mostly for beach and buffet. Unlike most Cuban resort areas, the town itself has a few entertainment, shopping and dining options.

Things to do in and around Varadero include enjoying beach and water sports activities, disco dancing, dolphin interaction, golf and various tours to local sights. Varadero with a few off-resort nightlife opportunities beats most of the other Cuban beach destinations.

VARADERO'S SIGHTS

There isn't much in the way of traditional sights. Here you go:

NATURE TOUR JEEP SAFARI
Jeeps come around to your hotel and take you on a day-long trip through the countryside with visits to Saturn Cave (see below) and Coral Beach. Activities include snorkeling, horseback riding, canoeing and walking along forested trails to see wildlife and birds. This is one of the more popular tours. *Info: Adult CUC 73, Child CUC 55 Cubatur, Avenida 1ra y 33. www.cubatur.cu; Tel. 45-66-7217.*

SATURNO CAVE
The cave is basically a large hole in the ground about half full of crystal-clear water. It's good for snorkeling and there are some galleries with stalactites and stalagmites for advanced scuba divers to explore. Blind shrimp inhabit the dark regions. *Info: On the turnoff to the airport.*

TOURS TO HAVANA
Cubatur offers several day and overnight tours to Havana. Their **Colonial Havana Tour** leaves Varadero in the morning and returns in time for dinner. A guided tour of Old Havana is the deal with lunch included. *Info:*

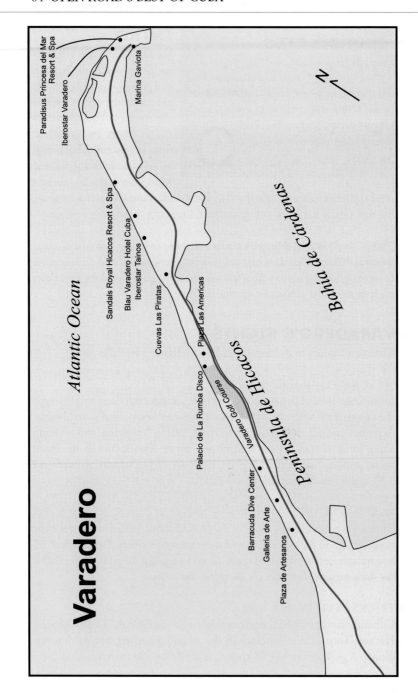

Adult CUC 67, Child CUC 51. Cubatur, Avenida 1ra y 33. www.cubatur.cu; Tel. 45-66-7217.

Their **Havana Special** tour gets you back late at night since, in addition to the standard tour of Havana, it also includes an evening at the famous Tropicana. Adults only. *Info: CUC 135. Cubatur, Avenida 1ra y 33. www.cubatur.cu; Tel. 45-66-7217.*

Bugs?

Varadero in general has plenty of mosquitoes. They have planes that spray noxious chemicals over all the hotels from time to time but it doesn't seem to help. There are plenty of flies, too so bring lots of DEET-containing bug spray.

BEST SLEEPS & EATS
Sleeps
Among the hotels in Varadero, **Club Puntarena**, **Hotel Internacional** and **Hotel Playa Caleta** are actual ocean front hotels (towers) right on the beach overlooking the beach and ocean. Almost all the other hotels are resort type properties that are set back from the beach a little but with some ocean view rooms. All the beaches in Varadero are spectacular. The hotels do not live up to their Cuban government star ratings. Subtract at least one star.

There are no legal private rooms in *casas particulares* for tourists in Varadero. You have to stay in one of the resorts. Keep in mind that the newest resorts are near the marina, the farthest away from the airport.

Paradisus Princesa del Mar Resort & Spa $$$$
Located almost at the end of the peninsula and a little smaller than some of the nearby resorts in the same class, the Paradisus is probably the nicest property in Varadero. It is an adults only resort aimed at a younger crowd.

Because of its location at the end of the beach, there are few other beach goers other than hotel guests and the beach in front of the resort is one of the least busy in Varadero.

The buffet is open-air

with no fans so it can get quite hot. The Japanese a-la-carte is my favorite of the four selections. There are 8 restaurants to choose from, Italian (not the best), Asian, French, Cuban, Japanese, beach restaurant, Racquet Club, and the main buffet. The Cuban restaurant is outdoors and usually stiflingly hot.

The swim-up bar is great but has a limited drink selection. The beach bar often cooks a huge paella for lunch.

Private salsa classes are a big hit. The evening "animation," as in many Cuban resorts, is extremely lame but the musicians in the restaurants and bars are very good. The Asian restaurant was fine when I was there. You sit at table of 6 with your own chef who cooks your food in front of you. Since the resort is adults only with mostly couples it is usually very quiet after 10pm except for the occasional "beach parties".

There are no actual five star quality hotels in Cuba. This isn't one either although British and Canadian travel agents frequently present it as such. *Info: km 19 1/2. www.meliacuba.com/cuba-hotels/hotel-paradisus-princesadelmar; Tel. 4-566-7200.*

Iberostar Varadero $$$$
The large, 326-room Iberostar is popular with the young singles party crowd. The hotel is a little on the run-down side but they have a bit more to do than the other resorts. Only a few of the rooms have any sort of sea view.

The white sand beach is long but fairly narrow so don't expect a huge, fancy, fancy beach. The water is shallow for a long way out so it is great for

swimming. Although the beach is narrow and somewhat diminished by recent storms, there is an effort underway to pump more sand onto the beach from just offshore. The resort has recently added 70 new beach umbrellas so there should be plenty of shade for beachgoers.

The hotel is known for their lively evening show. The small, air-conditioned disco is a good stop after the show if you feel like another drink or two.

Kayaks and pedaloes are available which can be great fun. There are daily snorkeling trips and the usual assortment of tours available.

Unusual for most all-inclusives, the buffet is probably a better bet most nights than the a-la-carte choices. I found the Japanese and Cuban (not air-conditioned) restaurants to be not so good but the seafood specialty restaurant was fine. The Mediterranean al la carte is air-conditioned! *Info: Carretera. Las Morlas, km. 16. www.iberostar.com/EN/Varadero/hotels-Varadero.html; Tel. 4-566-9999.*

Blau Varadero Hotel Cuba $$$$
I consider the Blau to be somewhat lacking in character even though it is supposed to resemble a Mexican pyramid. It is a bit of a high-rise with 12 floors and several hundred rooms. There are elevators (slow). Some rooms have a great ocean view.

Perhaps not actually a plus, there are always lots of birds with you for lunch in the poolside restaurant. It also doubles up as one of the a-la-cartes. There is always plenty of choice at lunch, for example burgers, sausages, salad, chips, pizza and various meats on the grill every day.

The pool is looking a little tired in terms of missing tiles and grout. A nice touch is that previous guests are acknowledged and invited to dinner with the manager. There is a tame piano bar on the same floor as the restaurant. The lunch grill is one of the a-la-carte choices for dinner – outside with the mosquitoes. The Palma Real a-la-carte is indoors and air-conditioned. The food is very well presented. The excellent strolling musicians will take requests. It's not really mentioned much but next to the bar downstairs they serve afternoon tea with biscuits (cookies) from 4pm-6pm. Get there

early if you want some biscuits. There is a very small cinema room and a rather smelly games room which has pool table, ping-pong, TV and board games. The beach is great and the staff are generally friendly and polite. *Info: Carretera de las Morlas, km. 15. www.blau-hotels-cuba.com. Tel. 4-566-7545.*

Sandals Royal Hicacos Resort & Spa $$$

Couples only, slightly dated and a bit worn looking, the Royal Hicacos is perhaps not the best of the Caribbean Sandals resorts but still attracts a large crowd of mostly younger couples and a few singles.

The large buffet is typical of Cuban resorts but not up to the same standards found in Sandals in other countries. The El Caribe is one of the better choices. The grill restaurant on the beach has good sunset views but you need to book it early to guarantee the best table. The Caribbean is another reasonable choice. The Don Pasquale Italian a-la-carte has good tiramisu and Las Morlas features seafood.

The evening shows are pretty corny as is usual in Cuban resorts but the magic show is spot on. The beach in front of the resort is wide with usually calm, clear water and it's shallow. You can wade out quite a long ways. There are plenty of shady spots on the beach. You can have all the scuba diving you want and for free. There is tennis and squash.

The Concierge Service, which includes a fruit plate, some sparkling wine, a couple of bottles of water and the ability to eat in the a-la-carte restaurants all week is probably not worth the extra CUCs but, if you have ever stayed at a Sandals before, be sure to tell them so you will be upgraded to the

dubious "Signature Guest" level—whatever that is. *Info: Carretera de Las Morlas km. 14. www.sandalshicacos.com; Tel. 4-566-8470.*

Iberostar Tainos $$$$
The Tainos is great for families with small children but it is getting a bit tired and in need of a refurb. Run down infrastructure and peeling paint are the most noticeable features. It is getting a bit long in the tooth with stained plaster, curtains falling down, and crumbling concrete walkways. The bungalows have the nicest rooms. The beach and grounds are great.

Eating and drinking options include Restaurant Sakura, Restaurant La Isabelica, Restaurant El Criollo, Pool Restaurant La Media Vuelta, Bar Playa Arena Fina, Pool Bar La Esquina, Lobby Bar La Palma, Bar Theatre Don Café del Iberostar Tainos, and Bar Ranchón La Duna. That's a lot of bars.

The lobby bar is nice but gets crowded in the evening as it is one of the few places where you can get a drink at night. The disco/entertainment bar is air-conditioned. Their web site is useful for checking room availability but has little other useful information. *Info: Km 12.5. www.iberostar.com; Tel. 4-566-8656.*

Eats

The resorts are all-inclusive with food and drink paid for in advance and there are not really many offsite choices of restaurants that are worth paying extra for. In town, in the **Parque de Las 8000 Taquillas**, there is a newish shopping center with **Copelia** selling their wonderful ice cream.

A Shot of Rum, Please

If you want to use a little bit of vernacular Spanish – ask for "*un trago*" – a gulp or shot when ordering rum. "*Muy rico!*" means "delicious!" and "*buen provecho*" means "have a nice meal.

Pizza Nova $$
Nova has a fair selection of standard pizza toppings and nice views from the balcony. Dough is rather like cardboard and the pepperoni is unlike any you may have seen in Italy—it resembles bologna more than anything else. If the kids are screaming

for pizza this will satisfy them. Avoid the pasta. *Info: Plaza América; Tel. 45-66-8585.*

La Campana $$$
A sort of hunting lodge themed place with stone fireplace and trophy heads on the walls watching you eat are highlights. Beef, pork and some seafood are on the very simple menu. *Info: Parque Josone. Tel. 45-66-7228.*

Lai Lai $$$
This is one of the better attempts at Chinese food I have tried in Cuba but still nothing like you would expect back home. You can order lobster chop suey. *Info: Avenida 1ra entre 18/19. Tel. 45-66-7793.*

Bodegón Criollo $$$
Rather expensive Cuban cooking with ropa vieja and other common *típico* meals including pork and chicken. *Info: Avenida Playa #40. Tel. 45-66-7784.*

BEST SHOPPING
Cigars and rum are usually cheaper at the airport duty-free than in the hotel shops. Across the street from the Meliá Las Americas is the scrummy Plaza Americas shopping mall where you can pick up some basic food and drink items.

Taller de Cerámica Artística
As the name implies, creative, decorative ceramics are what this store is all about. They feature hand painted individual plates and bowls as well as complete place settings with all the expected accouterments. *Info: Avenida 1ra y 59. Tel. 45-66-7554.*

Plaza de Artesanos
This is a small handicrafts market that, with Cuba's liberalizing private enterprise laws, is beginning to thrive and offer some interesting designs. The usual Che t-shirts are plentiful but they also have carved statues, fabrics, and some basic jewelry *Info: Avenida 1ra entre 15 y 16.*

Galleria de Arte
Paintings, wood carvings and handicrafts are a little bit more upscale in this gallery. *Info: Avenida 1ra y 59. Tel. 45-66-8260.*

BEST NIGHTLIFE & ENTERTAINMENT

Almost all the entertainment in Varadero is in the **resorts**. Nightly stage shows, *espectáculos*, can be lame, cheesy and amateurish but some of the acts are great. There is usually at least part of any of the shows that will be entertaining. The musicians are always excellent no matter what silly things the show designers have them doing.

Most of the resorts have a nightly disco and all have a bar or two open all night. In town, there are one or two places of interest.

Varadero is primarily a beach destination and most of the activities revolve around water sports in the day and music, drinking, and shows in the evenings. You can certainly visit resorts other than the one you are staying at in the evenings but, in my opinion, most of the shows are tacky and seem contrived.

LIVE MUSIC& DANCING
Almost all the live music you hear will be excellent. Some places more focused on dancing than live music can blast out ghastly reggaeton and Cubaton but that is true anywhere.

Palacio de La Rumba Disco

This is a regular old disco with DJs much like you might find in any country. The music is not really very Cuban but good for dancing. It is usually packed with tourists and locals who want to meet tourists. Drinks are cheap but service is slow and awkward. Pickpockets and robberies are common. DO NOT BRING A PURSE WITH YOU. Cover is CUC 10. Dress up. *Info: Carretera Las Américas, Km3.5; Tel. 45-66-8210.*

Cuevas Las Piratas

Situated in a small cave, this disco/cabaret plays hip-hop and reggaeton almost exclusively. There is a bit of a pirate theme with the waiters dressed up in silly outfits. Aargh matey! It's usually hot and sweaty. Drinks are fairly cheap but there is a CUC 10 cover charge. Some nights they have stage shows with dancers, singers and the usual novelty acts with the DJs afterwards. *Info: Avenida del Sur. Tel. 45-66-7751.*

Mambo Club

This venue is mostly for live music—mostly traditional Cuban but they put on the usual DJ stuff after the show. CUC 10 cover charge but drinks are included. *Info: Carretera Las Morlas next to Hotel Aguas Azules. Tel. 45-66-8565.*

SHOWS

Varadero has no shortage of *espectáculos*—elaborate stage shows with dancing girls, novelty acts and singers. I find these shows to be a bore but most visitors seem to love them.

La Comparsita

This large, open-air club has a fair stage show and live music beginning at about 11pm downstairs. Upstairs they have a disco with DJ and, in another room, karaoke. It is popular with tourists and a few locals who can afford the CUC 10 cover charge (all you can drink!) or who can talk a gringo to paying for them. *Info: Calle 60, esquina 3ra. Tel. 45-66-7415.*

Tropicana Varadero

The Tropicana in Varadero offers pretty much the same over-done *espectáculo* as do their locations in Havana and Santiago featuring dancing, music and fabulous costumes with lots of skin showing. I feel it's quite the tourist trap but almost everyone I ask says they loved the experience. Most of the resorts arrange for transportation to and from your hotel. *Info: Adult CUC49, Child, CUC 34.*

BEST SPORTS & RECREATION

DIVING & SNORKELING

There are numerous opportunities for snorkeling as part of the many organized tours including catamaran trips, cave snorkeling, and boat adventures. There are several marinas with diving centers and some resorts have their own facilities for guests.

The reefs offshore are very good but most boats tend to go to the same old spots over and over again leaving them a bit shopworn. If you are diving for several days and are willing to tip

Topless? Thongs?

Topless sunbathing and hanging around by the pool are not uncommon on Cuba's beaches and at the beach and buffet resorts. Europeans are the main culprits. They are usually fairly discrete—you don't see topless women prancing around. You will probably see thong bikinis at resort pools. If you are unsure, go ahead and pack your thong, since they don't take up much space in a suitcase, and check out the scene yourself before taking the plunge. Either topless or thonged, you will certainly receive appreciate stares from Cubans and other tourists.

generously, you may be able to lure your dive operator to take you to some of the more remote and less-visited sites.

The best dive sites are at least an hour boat ride from the docks around Varadero but the diving is good even at the closer, more frequently visited sites. There are several wrecks, walls and some caves/swim-throughs.

The dive operators charge pretty much the same: CUC 50 per dive with the option of multiple dive packages for less. Cuban company Marlin operates three marinas with dive centers. Gaviota's marina and dive center is at the far eastern end of the island.

Most of the all-inclusive resorts offer snorkeling trips and have snorkeling equipment available for guests.

Barracuda Diving Center
Operated by Marlin, ACUC dive certification courses are on offer as well as rentals of most types of water sports equipment. Daily scuba trips are usually two tank dives. The dive center organizes night dives if enough divers are interested. *Info: Avenida 1, Calle 8. Tel. 45-66-7072.*

Marina Gaviota
The Gaviota dive center is slightly cheaper than the others in town and they will pick you up and drop you off at your hotel for no extra charge. They offer ACUC courses for beginners and advanced. *Info: At the far eastern and of Autopista Sur. Tel. 44-66-7755.*

FISHING
Deep-sea fishing for billfish, dorado and tuna can be done from any of four marinas. Costs run from CUC 340 for a half day to CUC 600 for a full day for four anglers. Although this is not the best fishing area in Cuba, you are sure to have a good day out with the probability of catching something you can eat. Wahoo, tuna and billfish are the usual objectives.

Most hotels will book trips for you but you can also visit one of the marinas and sort out a trip for yourself. This way you can have a look at the boats and equipment before committing yourself.

There is not really much of an opportunity to hire a local fisherman to take you out in his small boat since most small boats are no longer in Cuba—

they are in Miami. There are not very many independent Cuban fishermen.

Marina Gaviota, (*Info: At the far eastern and of Autopista Sur. Tel. 45-66-4115.*), **Marlin Marina Chapelín** (*Info: Autopista Sur, Km 12. Tel. 45-66-8727.*), and **Marlin Marina Dársela** (*Info: Vía Blanca. Tel. 45-66-8060.*) are all full-service marinas hosting fishing charter boats as well as offering scuba trips and docking for passing yachties. Offshore fishing trips run about CUC 340 for a half day. The boats supply all the equipment needed and offer lunch and an open bar. Can't beat that.

CATAMARAN CRUISE
Seafari Crucero Del Sol
The popular catamaran cruise is one of the better things to do in Varadero. Schedules and places visited vary and your resort tour desk will have brochures with the highlights of each type of cruise detailed. Most cruises are all day and include snorkeling, a visit to the dolphinarium at Cayo Blanco, lobster lunch and open bar. They supply all the snorkeling equipment. *Info: Adult CUC 100, Child CUC 75.*

Of course, if you're handy with sailboats, take one out on your own from one of the resorts and enjoy a day on the water on your own.

SWIM WITH DOLPHINS
The popular dolphinarium is a government-run dolphin show and swim session. It's rather expensive. If a couple of adults and kids participate you can expect to drop $US 400 or more. They offer pick up and drop off at the hotels. If you are near the front during the show you are very likely to get soaking wet. When swimming with the dolphins, make sure you wear a bathing suit that does not come off easily. The show is good but the water is cloudy. The DVD for CUC 35 is definitely not worth it. *Info: Show Only CUC 15, Adult Swim CUC 89, Child Swim CUC 67.*

GOLF
Varadero Golf Club
Book at the pro shop next to the DuPont Mansion. CUC 80 for 18 holes. CUC 55 to rent clubs and CUC 30 for the cart (per person) but you get it for all day. The word is the government plans to make investments into the quality of the course. Look for new greens in 2012. There is no enforcement of the booking system so there can be confusion about who is playing when. Tee times are meaningless. Whoever shows up first tees off whenever they feel like it. *Info: Carretera Las Morlas. Tel. 45-66-7788.*

SKYDIVING
People may approach you on the beach offering to book you for skydiving. They drop from 10,000 feet and you land on the beach in front of your resort. Cool. CUC 200 if you are certified and CUC 250 for a tandem jump. CUC 50 for the DVD of your adventure. Last I heard they are using a helicopter to drop people from 10,000 ft. Sweet! **Centro Internacional de Paracaidismo** *Info: In the old Kawama airport, Carretera Vía Blanca, Km 1 1/2. www.cubairsports.itgo.com; Tel. 5-66-7256.*

6. SANTIAGO DE CUBA

HIGHLIGHTS

▲ Visit Casa de la Trova for traditional Cuban Music

▲ Wallow in Carnival

▲ Visit historic sights and museums

▲ Have a drink at the rooftop bar at the Hotel Casa Granda

▲ Prowl the picturesque streets of the colonial district

COORDINATES

Located about 450 miles from Havana on the southeastern part of the island, **Santiago** is one of Cuba's liveliest cities. Flights from Havana can cost about US$300 and take about two hours. Overland by bus, car or train can take at least two days.

INTRO

Santiago has a great old center, the colonial district, in the neighborhood around **Parque Céspedes**. It is a good area for walking, checking out the colonial architecture, listening to authentic Cuban music, and stopping here and there for a beer. You can easily spend a day or more doing this. Having a drink or meal on the roof terrace at the **Hotel Casa Granda Santiago de Cuba** is a good way to get the 1950s Humphrey Bogart feeling stirring in your soul. It's a beautiful city center.

While smaller than Havana, Santiago is still a huge city. Fortunately, most of the places of interest to visitors are near the center of town. Just outside town are some reasonable waterfront resorts and there is a scenic drive along the coast to the west.

The city and surrounding areas are full of historic sites. Many significant revolutionary actions took place in the vicinity including the famous **Moncada Barracks** attack. Many visitors come just for the history lessons. Santiago is also **Cuba's top music town**. Home to the **Casa de La Trova** and many of the original **Buena Vista Social Club** members. There are literally dozens of places to go for great son, timba, rumba and salsa. What a scene for music lovers!

Santiago is justly famous for its fanciful **Carnival** celebration held in July. The opening weekend of the weeklong celebration involves a parade and fireworks display. Large parts of the city are blocked off for street parties with live music and DJs. Street stalls sell sometimes dodgy food and a special carnival beer—bring your own container—for about US$ 0.10 for a liter. The festivities go on in pretty much the same fashion for the rest of the week.

SANTIAGO'S SIGHTS

Santiago is loaded with museums and holy spots from the revolution. It would take several days to visit just the best museums and historical sights.

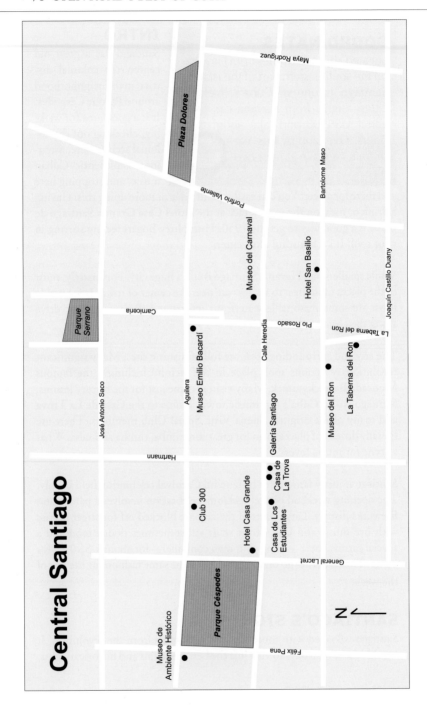

Central Santiago

Museo de Ambiente Histórico

Parque Céspedes

Félix Pena

General Lacret

Hotel Casa Grande

Club 300

Casa de Los Estudiantes

Casa de La Trova

Galería Santiago

José Antonio Saco

Hartmann

Aguilera

Museo Emilio Bacardí

Parque Serrano

Carnicería

Calle Heredia

Pío Rosado

Museo del Carnaval

Museo del Ron

La Taberna del Ron

Hotel San Basilio

Bartolome Maso

Joaquín Castillo Duany

Porfirio Valiente

Plaza Dolores

Maya Rodríguez

N

San Pedro de la Roca del Morro Castle

Just a little ways outside town (9 miles) you shouldn't miss **World Heritage Site** San Pedro de la Roca el Morro Castle (*see photo on page 76*). The old fort on a rocky promontory far along the scenic Carretera del Morro is now a pirate museum. It was supposed to keep pirates out of the port but failed at this. Don't miss it if you have kids.

Lobster with a View

Next to el Morro, there is a more interesting than usual place to eat where you can get shrimp, lobster, fancy cocktails and the like. The food is expensive but the view is tremendous. The rumor is that Paul McCartney stopped in and used the bathroom here once. Or something.

The fortress, **El Morro**, was designed by the same guy, Italian Juan Bautista Antonelli, who designed the one guarding Havana's harbor. It was built in the 1630s. It's huge and in a truly cool setting and it is worth tramping around in and taking pictures for an hour or so. Kids will love the included **Museo de Piratería**, Pirate Museum. They do a sundown cannon-firing display most nights with gunners dressed up in period outfits. Very cool. *Info: Carretera del Morro, km. 8. Open daily 8am-7pm. CUC 4. Tel. 22-69-1569.*

Cuartel Moncada

On July 26th, 1953, Castro and his band attacked this castle-like barracks in a futile attempt to spark the inevitable revolution. The attack failed spectacularly but, several years later, Fidel and his men succeeded with their revolution and the audacity of the fighters is legendary. **Moncada Barracks** is of supreme historical significance for Cubans and is a popular destination for tourists from all over the world. Perhaps the most important revolutionary site in Cuba, this is where Fidel launched his first guerilla attack against the state.

There is a museum inside loaded with historical artifacts. See carefully preserved bloody uniforms, old weapons and other items of historical interest. The authorities have authentically recreated bullet holes in the walls for tourist photos. *Info: Avenida de Los Libertadores. Tuesday-Saturday 9:30am – 5:15pm. Sunday 9am – noon. CUC 2. Tel. 22-62-0157.*

Museo de Ambiente Histórico

Once the house of the viceroy Diego Velásquez, the Museo de Ambiente

Histórico is now a museum displaying artifacts from the history of Cuba. Music *peñas*, clubs, meet here in the mornings and for performances on Wednesday, Thursday, Saturday and Sunday. *Info: Casa Velázquez, Felix Peña 612, corner of Calle Aguilera and Calle Felix. Open daily 9am-1pm and 2-5pm. Tel. 22-65-2652.*

Museo del Carnaval
The museum aims to give an overview of the great tradition of carnival in Santiago. *Info: Heredia 303, esquina Pío Rosado. Tues-Sat 9am-8pm; Sun 9am-5pm. Tel. 22-62-6955.*

Museo Emilio Bacardí
This was one of Cuba's first museums, set up by Emilio Bacardí, and built by architect Carlos Segrera. It houses a valuable collection of fine art and antiquities covering the period between the Spanish conquest and the Wars of Independence. There is an Egyptian mummy. This is a nice museum. *Info: Pío Rosado y Aguilera. 3pm-8pm Mon; 9am-9pm Tue-Sat; 9am-4pm Sun. CUC 1.*

Museo del Ron
The museum has everything you always wanted to know about rum with displays of machinery, interesting old bottles, and historical photographs. One free shot of rum comes with the tour. The museum is in a beautiful old house that used to belong to the Bacardi family. *Info: Monday – Saturday 9am – 5pm. CUC 20. Esquina Calle Hartmann (San Félix) and Calle Castillo Duany (Santa Lucía).*

Museo de la Clandestinidad (Museum of the Underground Struggle)
Yet another shrine to the revolutionary effort, the museum purportedly contains memorabilia relevant to the underground struggle including a couple of Molotov cocktails. It is located in an interesting replica of an old mansion, **Loma del Intendente,** that used to be police headquarters. It was burned down during the revolution but rebuilt for purposes of historical pride. There are lots of old photographs of the Batista era. Fidel once lived across the street. *Info: Tues-Sun 9am-5pm. CUC 1. Jesus Rabí 1 between Santa Rita and San Carlos. Tel. 22-62-4689.*

Loma de San Juan
This is the hill that Teddy Roosevelt and his Rough Riders stormed up to defeat Spanish troops. *Info: Reparto Santa Bárbara, esquina Avenida de Raúl*

Pujol and Carretera de Siboney Km 1.5 (next to the Hotel Horizontes San Juan).

BEST SLEEPS & EATS
Sleeps
Santiago has no fine hotels although there are several good *casas particulares*, rooms officially available in private homes. Several of the city's hotels are loaded with character and were quite elegant many years ago. I suggest two hotels in town and two all-inclusives just outside town. I also mention a newly renovated boutique hotel and three *casas particulares*.

Hotel Casa Granda Santiago de Cuba $$$
Not much is grand about it anymore but the location right on Carlos Manuel de Céspedes Park close to the tourist attractions is extremely convenient as a base for exploring the town. The hotel has Santiago's most famous terrace overlooking Santiago's most famous square and cathedral and is certainly one of the old great hotels of Santiago. Even though it was recently renovated it is in need of a lot of work to be said to be truly "comfortable". It's loud and overpriced. The old-fashioned rooms are mostly huge with high ceilings and large bathrooms hinting at the overall elegance that was once here.

Rooms facing the square have a great view but may be noisy. Other rooms facing the interior courtyard should be quieter.

Its best features are the lobby and rooftop bars. Try them both. Whenever there is something going on in the square, the rooftop bar gives you the best views. The lobby bar on the downstairs patio serves snacks and also has a good view of the square. I like to rest in the rooftop bar with a cold beer after walking my feet off exploring town. The restaurant itself is uninteresting but serves up a reasonable meal. The restaurant usually has excellent live music in the evenings.

Info: Calle Heredia 201 entre San Pedro y San Félix. www.hotelcasagranda.com; Tel. 7-864-9177.

Meliá Santiago de Cuba $$$

With no frills and well over-priced, this is the probably best in hotel in Santiago. The rooms are a bit run-down and the five restaurants are too expensive by far. There are nice views from some of the higher up rooms.

They have three pools, one with a decent bar. The hotel is plain from the outside like a dreary 15 story office building. It's about two kilometers from the city center. There are lots of cabs hanging about and fewer beggars/hustlers than in the city center. The place seems stuck back in time, about 1955 or so. The food and general staff attitude are both poor. *Info: Avenida. de Las Américas y Calle M. www.meliacuba.com; Tel. 22-68-7070.*

Hotel San Basilio $$$

The San Basilio is a recently renovated boutique hotel with eight rooms in lovely old building with AC but no pool. It's nicely located on a back street just a block or two from the action. Some of the rooms are noisy. Stray cats sometimes invite themselves into your room. It's a nice little place close in. *Info: Calle San Basilio No 403 e/ Ca. Tel. 22-65-1702.*

Gran Caribe Club Bucanero $$$

An all-inclusive resort, just outside Santiago, the Bucanero gets mixed reviews from people I talk to. The ropa vieja at the buffet is said to be brilliant but that's about all the positive comments I have heard. The beach is rather small but the snorkeling is good. Most rooms have a view of the ocean. The hotel is about a half hour ride into the city.

The pool bar is open 24/7 but the bartender may be asleep. No problem. The snack bar at the beach has the best food in the place: fried chicken and grilled fish, hot dogs, hamburgers and fries. The a-la-carte restaurants have the same food as the buffet—just served more slowly. Rumors are a major renovation may be coming in 2012. *Info: Carretera de Baconao, Km 4. www.gran-caribe.com/english/hotel.asp?hotel_code=SCTGCBucanero; Tel. 7-864-9177.*

Club Amigo Carisol Los Corales $$

The resort consists of two hotels: Los Corales and the Club Amigo Carisol, and neither get high marks for quality. The resort has a large private beach which both hotels share. The beach is a little rocky for swimming but good for snorkeling. There is also a public beach beside Los Corales.

The rooms are reasonably comfortable but are known for interesting plumbing and dodgy AC. They have the usual large buffets, a pizza restaurant, a pool bar, a lobby bar and a beach bar. A few goats wander around leaving droppings on the tennis courts—no problem.

They offer all sorts of water sports with free catamaran rides, kayaks and peddle boats. There is windsurfing, a banana and a dive center. You can rent scooters. *Info: Carretera de Baconao, Kilometer 10.*

Casa Vilma y Peter $$

A casa particular close to of the center of things, this is a good choice. Peter speaks good English and can help with information about the area. Vilma is an excellent cook and will accommodate your preferences if you choose to eat there—a good idea. The rooms are clean but a little small. AC works fine and there is plenty of hot water. *Info: CUC 25 per room with breakfast. Trinidad (General Portuondo) No. 159 entre Gallo (Diez de Octubre) y San Pío (B.H. Vázquez). www.casa-vilma-y-peter.de; Tel. 53-22-62-3315.*

Casa Alejandro Thomas $$

Nice casa particular with third-floor rooms with a shared terrace. The owners will provide breakfast, lunch or dinner as you request. The food is wonderful home cooking—very Cuban. *Info: Calle Aguilera 682.*

Casa Leonardo y Rosa $$

In a beautiful old building, nicely maintained, this casa is close to the action but quiet (except for the roosters) with AC, fridge and two modern rooms. The bathrooms have been remodeled and the beds are nice. Rosa can prepare wonderful home-cooked meals on request. *Info: Calle Clarin 9.*

Eats

Unfortunately, there are only a few *Paladars,* privately run restaurants, in town, so you will mostly have to rely on state-run restaurants. This means you are probably going to be disappointed with your meals unless you are a real bottom-feeder. For a reasonable price, you can count on *casas particulares* to cook up the best meals in town. The upstairs restaurant in the Hotel Casa Granda at least overlooks the square and usually has excellent live music in the evenings.

El Salon Tropical $$

One of the few paladars in town, this is a good one. It has, without doubt, the best food and service in Santiago and is almost always busy. Call ahead for reservations. It is a rooftop place on a small street near the Meliá Santiago open for lunch and dinner. I suggest you eat most of your meals here. If you find anything better, please let me know. *Info: Fernández Marcané #310 Altos; Tel. 53-2264-1161.*

El Morro

Touristy but interesting anyway, El Morro is near town on the coast by the old fort called, coincidentally, El Morro. Food is more interesting than in most state-run restaurants but the service is typically slow. You can get lobster, shrimp and fancy cocktails. Expensive but the view is great. *Info: Carretera del Morro, km. 8. Tel. 53-22-69-1576.*

Las Gallegas Paladar

In a nice old building with a view of the street, a family of four sisters has been serving up their lamb specialty for several years in spite of the country's economic ups and downs. *Info: Bartelome Maso #305 altos, e/ General Lacret and San Félix, Centro Historico. Tel. 53-22-62-4700.*

Zunzun

Of fading reputation but still more or less classy, Zunzun is still perhaps the most elegant eatery in Santiago. White tablecloths aside, the food quality and service can vary. The place is famous for its ups and downs. International shellfish is supposed to be the theme (lobster) but reasonable beefsteaks are also on the menu. Expensive but sophisticated! *Info: Ave Manduley #159 esquina. 7, Vista Alegre. Tel. 53-22-64-1369.*

BEST SHOPPING

As in almost all of Cuba, shopping is pretty sparse. Rum, cigars, Che T-shirts, caps with the Cuban flag on them, and various tourist-oriented trinkets are about all you will find. That said; look for the occasional painting by local artists. Some of these are stunningly good.

Casa de La Trova
Next to the famous music venue, the store has a reasonable variety of CDs, many from local artists. A few musical instruments round out the offerings. *Info: Heredia #208.*

El Quitrín
Well-tailored men and women's clothes are made in the old house. If you are looking for a good-quality guayabera, this is a good place to start. *Info: San* Gerónimo.

Galería Santiago
An art gallery with a large display of paintings by locals, the Galería has some handicrafts. *Info: Heredia #208.*

BEST NIGHTLIFE & ENTERTAINMENT
Music lovers come to Santiago to soak up the best music in Cuba. Museum and historical site visits, drives out of town along the coast are also good options. For me, Santiago is a night town. Party lovers find **Carnival** in Santiago to be one of the most interesting in the Caribbean. I come mostly for the chance to hear great music—some young and upcoming performers as well as established greats.

Santiago is famous as the birthplace and nursery for some of Cuba's greatest musicians. Some of the greats are still around and playing and some fantastic new talent is making their own scene.

Some venues have afternoon shows at a lower price. You have to kind of ask around a bit to find out who is playing where.

WATERING HOLES
It's nice to have a couple of favorite bars to hang out in waiting for pals or just cooling off. Most of these below have good live music most nights and often in the afternoon.

La Taberna del Ron
Underneath the Museo de Ron, the Taberna sells shots of good-quality

rum for CUC 1. What a deal! It's on the small side but not usually very crowded at night. *Info: Bartolome Maso #358.*

Club 300
Small and dark, there are live performances every weekend night and often during the week. It's a fairly young crowd. No cover charge. *Info: Aguilera #300.*

Hotel Casa Granda Terrace Bar
I like to have a couple of beers here while watching the action on the square below. Makes me feel like Humphrey Bogart or something. The bar is in the fading but still charming old 50s-style hotel Casa Granda. It's a great bar with a wonderful view. Too bad about the service. *Info: Calle Heredia 201* entre San Pedro y San Félix. *www.gran-caribe.com; Tel. 7-864-9177.*

Bello Bar
On the 15th floor of the Meliá Santiago, the bar has wonderful views and pretends to be swanky. They have 2 for 1 happy hour from 7pm to 8pm. The show at 10pm is usually crummy and easily skipped but on Saturday nights they have a highly entertaining fashion show. *Info: Avenida de Las Américas y Calle M.*

LIVE MUSIC VENUES
There is live music all over the place. You can hear excellent bands in corner bars and cafes as well as in nightclubs and shows. There is no shortage of live music in Santiago. You can start at Casa de La Trova where you are likely to hear great music at almost any time of day.

Casa de La Trova
Famous all over the world as a hotbed of the best Cuban music, there are musical performances almost every afternoon and evening. The quality is

always good and sometimes some truly greats perform. This is should be number one on almost anyone's list of things to do in Santiago. I love it. There are usually lots and lots of tourists but so what? Son, trova, boleros—this is the real thing. *¡Muy auténtico! Info: 208 Heredia. Tel. 22-65-2689.*

Casa de Los Estudiantes
With traditional music performances in the mornings, ballet in the afternoon and rockin' salsa bands in the evenings there's always something worth listening to. *Info: Heredia #204 next to Casa de La Trova.*

SHOWS
Cubans love their *espectáculos* (spectacular shows) and Santiago has its share. Some folks love the spectacular costumes, exotic dances, long legs, magicians and cheesy skits. Food is usually dire and service difficult. Still, it's an unforgettable night out.

Cabaret Tropicana Santiago $$$$
Much like its sister in Havana, and the second largest show in Cuba, this is, in my opinion, simply a tourist trap and a money-sucking machine (seats 850). However I meet many people who absolutely love their experience at the Tropicana. The entertainment is much more elaborate than what you see on the concrete stage in every cheesy resort in Cuba. Whoever designs the sets, costumes and dance routines has been watching waaay too much MTV. Or something.

Food is included but I suggest you eat before you go and simply pass on the food. Waiters are typically difficult to flag down and frequently never return with your drink order. Check your bill carefully at the end of the night. *Info: km 11/2 Autopista Nacional, Santiago de Cuba. Tel. 53-22-68-7020.*

Casa de La Música
A very lively late night show, this is one of the main places in Santiago to see the major bands. There is lots of dancing and disco-like stuff but the live music is almost always excellent. There are always a herd of *jineteras*, young ladies look-

ing for a man hanging about. Doors open at 10pm but bands do not usually go on stage much before 1am and the live bands often do one disappointingly short set. Most people I talk to love the place but I find it to not be worth the trouble. It is similar to the Casas de La Música in Havana but not nearly as crowded. *Info: Corona #564. CUC 5. Tel. 53-22-62-3943.*

La Maison

La Maison is well known for their outdoor fashion/dance show. It is open nightly, 10pm weather permitting. This may sound like a lame scene but, if you are in the right mood, it can be a great night out. It's not as intense as the Tropicana. *Info: Manduley #52. Tel. 22-64-1117.*

Meliá Santiago de Cuba

On Saturday night the best show in town is the fashion/dance show at the "Cafe Meliá." Fashion shows are a popular Cuban stage event that some enjoy hugely. Plan on arriving about 9:30pm. *Info: Avenida. de las Américas y Calle M. www.solmelia.com; Tel. 22-68-7070.*

BEST SPORTS & RECREATION
DIVING & SNORKELING

Although the area around Santiago is not known as a prime dive destination, there is excellent scuba and snorkeling.

Los Corales has a dive shop with equipment in good order and offers usually a morning, two-tank dive for CUC 40. Reefs are in good condition with much less traffic than the ones visitors are usually taken to around Varadero and Cayo Coco.

Carisol Los Corales

The dive center at Carisol Los Corales is right on the beach. Their equipment is in reasonable condition and there are very good walls, wrecks and reefs. Trips usually leave everyday at 11am and cost CUC 40 per dive. You can book several at a reduced price. You can also just snorkel. They visit 27 marked dive sites including El Ferri, El Sprint, Carol, El Guárico, Coral Garden, and Morrillo. *Info: Carretera de Baconao, Kilometer 10.*

Marina Marlin

South of town about 6 miles is the Marina Marlin which offers a variety of water sports including scuba and snorkeling trips to the nearby reefs. They dive about 20 sites including Los Cajizotes and El Oquendo. *Info: Punta Gorda, Carretera Turística. www.nauticamarlin.com; Tel. 22-69-1446.*

FISHING
Marina Marlin offer fishing expeditions. Fishing tends to be near shore trolling and you can expect to catch, dolphin, tuna, jacks, wahoo, kingfish and barracuda.

Marina Marlin
Most tackle is available for basic trolling and spin casting. Fly fishermen will need to bring almost all their own equipment. The marina is about 6 miles outside Santiago. *Info: Punta Gorda, Carretera Turística. www.nauticamarlin.com; Tel. 22-69-1446.*

BIRDING
Driving east from Santiago along the coasty towards **Baconao** offers a multitude of birding opportunities. Many endemics can be seen including Cuban blackbird, Cuban mockingbird, Cuban grassquit, Cuban gnatcatcher (*see photo below*), Cuban vireo, Cuban tody and oriente warbler.

7. THE NORTHERN CAYS

HIGHLIGHTS
▲ Take long walks on white sand beaches

▲ Gorge on bountiful buffets

▲ Luxuriate in luxurious pools

▲ Give yourself up to naff resort activities

▲ Explore the nearby wilderness, birds and wildlife

COORDINATES

Deep blue ocean and white sand beaches border the north side of the cayos and mangroves and shallow flats separate the islands from the mainland. You can easily fly from Havana for about US$100.

INTRO

Cuba's prime beach destinations on the north coast, Cayo Coco, Cayo Guillermo and Cayo Santa Maria make up the Jardines del Rey (gardens of the king), the area Hemingway wrote about in his last novel *Islands in the Stream*. Further to the east, **Guardalavaca** is another of Cuba's best beach destinations.

Beach and buffet lovers find the **long, white sand beaches** and **cheap package prices** irresistible. There are at least 20 all-inclusive resorts from budget to approaching luxury to choose from. Canadians, Brits come in the winter months and South Americans come in the summer months (their wintertime).

The cayos are beautiful destinations. Even though there are numerous resorts, the low islands seem sparsely developed. Most of the water around the cayos is shallow with good fishing, scuba diving, snorkeling, sailing and all the usual beach activities.

The cayos have miles of wonderful beaches and you can always find a deserted area for walking.

With the success of Mexico's Cancun in mind, the Cuban government has been developing the cayos as tourism destinations. There are now a couple of dozen resorts on the cayos, an international airport and numerous tours and activities available to tourists. Long causeways with gates to control access separate the islands from the mainland.

Located on Cuba's north shore, far to the east end of the island, **Guardalavaca** offers one of the nicer beach destinations. It is further south than the resorts in the Cayos and Varadero and can be warm in the winter when cold fronts come through and chill the tourists further to the north. In a country with hundreds of great beaches, Guardalavaca is no slouch.

These are very quiet vacation spots. There are hardly any nightclubs, bars or restaurants to check out other than the ones at the other nearby all-inclusives. Since no one is actually allowed to live on the cayos, there are no local villages to visit. This is a place to enjoy the resort: pool, beach, evening entertainment and adult beverages. The beaches are astonishing. Be sure to bring plenty of high strength mosquito repellant. No-see-ums can also be battled with DEET.

NORTHERN CAY SIGHTS

Gaviota and **Cubatur** organize most of the activities for the hotels. Most activities seem to be designed primarily for extracting tourist dollars from tourist pockets with little thought to actually making them interesting or worthwhile. Most tours mentioned here are similar to tours offered in other tourist areas of Cuba but a couple are pretty cool.

Cayo Coco, Cayo Guillermo
Salsa Night
In case you can't figure out how to do it on your own, you can book this all-adults tour to a "local" disco at El Pueblo for salsa and drinks. Not surprisingly, the tour also includes a stop for cigar rolling. You get dinner, dance lessons and not much else for CUC 35. You can do it on your own without the cigar rolling for half the price and have a better dinner at your resort.

Jeep Safari
A holiday in Cuba would not be complete without a "Jeep Safari." All the

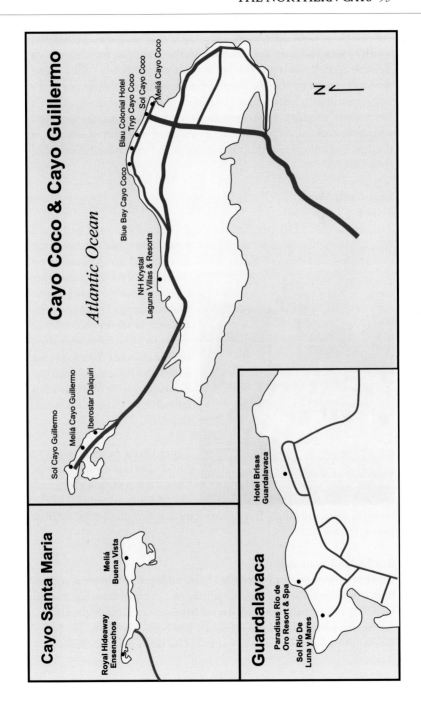

resort areas in Cuba offer them. I suppose it is a "must do". This all day activity takes you over the causeway to the mainland for a short ride through agricultural areas. You get to see farms producing coffee, sugarcane and you pass through a couple of small villages. A stop at one of the villages includes a rather lame "rodeo," a chance to swim in a river, a "traditional" meal in a country restaurant (government run, of course) and a welcome cocktail. A short look at the village of Remedios is also part of the deal. For some reason this trip is billed as "A Real Cuban Experience!" *Info: CUC 70.*

Cayo Santa María
Trinidad Town Tour
Trinidad, a World Heritage Site, is indeed a beautiful city and well worth

a visit. About half or more of the all day tour involves riding on the bus—Trinidad is on the other side of the island. A lunch stop at Manaca-Iznaga Tower gives you a chance to admire the Valley of the Sugar Mills, colonial squares, and old churches. You also visit a potter and the artisan's market. A meager lunch of sandwiches resembling Spam is included. *Info: CUC 75.*

Topes Forest Adventure
An all day trip through one of Cuba's few remaining forest areas includes naturalist guide, waterfall swim and lunch. It is a pretty long day with substantial walking. *Info: CUC 60.*

Key Seafari Catamaran
Catamaran trips are always popular. Some trips include dolphin interaction, snorkeling, open bar, lobster dinner or a combination. For around CUC 90 per person you get an all-day sail around a wreck, the dolphinarium, snorkeling, lobster lunch and open bar. The boats leave from Las Brujas Marina but a bus will come to your resort for the transfer (included).

Sunset Catamaran Cruise
Also leaving from Marina Las Brujas, the sunset catamaran sail lasts about four hours and includes lobster dinner and open bar. CUC 60. There are also wedding, overnight and "special" cruises available.

Cienfuegos Delfinarium
This is your regular old dolphin bashing show. For CUC 115 you get to see the trainers feeding the dolphins in return for some mild jumping through hoops and then you get to sit in the water with the dolphins and touch them a bit. This is called the "interactive swim." Not worth it.

Santa Clara, Remedios Tour
An all-day tour through the town of Santa Clara and Remedios, the tour includes the inevitable a stop at the Che Guevara museum, a cigar factory visit and lunch. Santa Clara is a plain Cuban town with little of interest but at least you do get to see how Cubans live as you drive around. *Info: CUC 70.*

Santa Clara Baseball Game
Now this is a good tour. Cuban baseball is nothing short of spectacular with international-quality play. The tour takes you from your resort by bus, gets you to the stadium and provides you with two beers and a snack, which is two beers and one snack more than anyone else will be getting at the game. You also get a guided tour of the stadium and may even get to meet some of the players. Even if you are not a baseball fan I suggest this as a good way to actually rub shoulders with some Cubans and witness their enthusiasm for the national sport. *Info: CUC 35.*

Guardalavaca
Thomas Cook Dolphin Tours
If you simply must swim with captive dolphins, Thomas Cook offers several options. All involve a trip across Bahia Naranja to the dolphinarium. There are three variations available. Many of the options involve an extra charge.

The basic dolphin excursion involves a trip by speedboat to the dolphinarium where you are welcomed by a groovy Cuban band and a free welcome cocktail. You then spend about 20 minutes in the water with the dolphins where you get to kiss and cuddle the frisky creatures.

There is a fairly standard sea lion/dolphin show with lots of jumping and splashing the audience. For extra CUCs you can be pulled around the pool a bit. Photographs and videos on DVD of your outing are always available (for extra CUCs). A stripped-down swim and show can be done for slightly less. Another option offered for about the same price involves a lobster dinner. Also for about CUC 100, you can combine a catamaran snorkeling tour, seafood lunch and dolphin swim. That tour is on Sundays only. *Info: Book through your resort's tour desk. Operates daily. Adults CUC 99, children CUC 48. Observers CUC 40 and CUC 20.*

Thomas Cook Jeep Tour

Almost all the resort areas in Cuba offer what is called a "jeep tour." Some are much better than others but all involve some fairly cheesy tours of uninteresting villages with bored "inhabitants" or visits to concrete monuments to obscure events in the revolution.

The jeep tour offered in the **Guardalavaca** area consists of riding around in an open-top jeep, horseback riding, jet skiing, ride on an ox, eating lunch at the beach where Columbus may have landed and visits to concrete "authentic" Cuban villages. Most people seem to like these excursions but I find them to be a crushing bore. *Info: Book through your resort's tour desk. Operates daily. CUC 49.*

The Grand Safari

I'm not sure how the word "safari" gets into the picture since you don't get to see any wildlife other than whatever buzzards happen to fly by. This trip is billed as your chance to "see the real Cuba." You drive around the farming areas of Holguin Provence, visit Fidel's birthplace, visit a small waterfall and a couple of fruit and flower plantations. You also get a cup of "traditional" Cuban coffee. I suppose this is not to be missed. *Info: Book through your resort's tour desk. Adults CUC 89, children CUC 64.*

The Great Adventure

On this tour you drive around the countryside in an open-topped jeep, eat lunch in the small fishing town of Gibara and do some jet skiing. I guess it's worth it. *Info: Book through your resort's tour desk. Adults CUC 74, children CUC 49.*

Cuba Inside

If you want to visit a fairly typical, small Cuban city, this is a good trip. You get to ride on an old steam engine through the sugarcane fields and visit the city of Holguin to see a cigar factory. You get some free time to wander around Cathedral Square and the city center. *Info: Book through your resort's tour desk. Adults CUC 59, children CUC 36.*

Santiago by Day

This is a long, long day trip but, in my opinion, one of the better tours going. You go straight to Santiago, one of the most fascinating towns in Cuba. You get a quick tour around town, lunch, an alcoholic drink, and time to explore on your own. Travel time is about three hours each way. *Info: Book through your resort's tour desk. Adults CUC 62, children CUC 42.*

Santiago Overnight

Another good tour, this one involves a long drive to Santiago, Cuba's Nashville—music city. On the way, you visit Bayamo and the Basilica El Cobre. In Santiago you make the obligatory stop at a couple of historic sites: Moncada Garrison where Fidel lost his first battle in 1953 and Revolution Square. You get a trip to Morro Fortress in the bay and, for an extra CUC 20 charge, an evening at the famous Tropicana to see the elaborate stage show complete with dancing girls covered in glitter. No children are allowed to attend the Tropicana show. *Info: Book through your resort's tour desk. Adults CUC 159, children CUC 64.*

Holguin by Night

This tour takes you to the nearby city of Holguin for a cabaret show and dancing. All the rum you can choke down is included. The show is a little bit lame but the music is great and the rum just fine. *Info: Book through your resort's tour desk. Adults CUC 25.*

Cuba Life

This is an easy tour of nearby banana plantations with a stop in Canadon town, the fishing village of Sama and some free time in the town of Guardalavaca. Lunch by the sea is included. Lobster is extra but still a good deal. *Info: Book through your resort's tour desk. Adults CUC 34, children 24 CUC.*

Natural Farmer

This tour is a rather odd combination of fishing, horseback riding, visit to a rodeo in Rocazul Biopark and visiting a rural farm. You get lunch and a hat. *Info: Book through your resort's tour desk. Adults CUC 39, children 19 CUC.*

BEST SLEEPS & EATS
Sleeps
CAYO COCO

Cayo Coco has at least a dozen all-inclusive resorts with Meliá Cayo Coco and Sol Cayo Coco (*see photo on page 90*) being the best of the lot—and they are nice. All of the resorts are on wonderful beaches. Due to wave action and the occasional hurricane, the state of the beaches changes. The beaches in this area are almost always wide, white sand with some small areas of weed in the shallows. Some resorts are more private than others but all are a short walk to other resorts.

Meliá Cayo Coco $$$$

Generally rated as the top resort on the northern cays, everything about the Meliá is "good" but nothing is really "great." The Italian restaurant is the best of the a-la-carte choices even if the lasagna is frozen. The buffet food is typical about the same as in all the Cuban resorts—only fair, or "okay" and bland. Rooms are fine but seem dated. Service is typically good but spotty depending on whom you deal with. The beach, although a bit narrow, is stunning. You can walk for hours on the beach, especially to the east and see almost no one. To the west the beach is shallow and wide but lined with the beach chairs of neighboring resorts. *Info: www.solmeliacuba.com; Tel. 53-33-30-1180.*

Sol Cayo Coco $$$

This is one of the nicer resorts in the Cayo Coco area. The white sand beach is great stretching for a mile or more in each direction. Although some of the bedrooms and other facilities are maybe a little tired, overall the resort

provides all the things necessary for a great vacation. There is a large pool and palm trees shade the grounds. Staff is generally friendly and responsive. The buffet is large enough so anyone can find a few favorite items at each meal. The pizza bar lines can be quite long. The dining room is enclosed and air-conditioned. There is a screened-in outside dining area. The al-la-carte restaurants are nice but be sure to make your reservations the first day or two of your stay. Most of the visitors are middle-aged couples some with small children. *Info: www.solmeliacuba.com; Tel. 53-33-30-1180.*

Blue Bay Cayo Coco $$$

The Blue Bay is a mid-range resort catering to couples and family holidays. A nice feature is the air-conditioning in the dining room. The sand on the beach is like flour and the ocean is deep blue. The beach is wonderful and quite shallow for a long way out. Cayo Coco has some herds of wild cattle running around and some stroll through the hotel grounds from time to time, dropping loads wherever it suits them. Nearby mangroves make for a mosquito issue. *Info: Cayo Coco. www.bluebayresorts.com; Tel. 53-33-30-1280.*

Blau Colonial Hotel $$$$

There are really two beaches here. The one to the left of the hotel can be a bit grainy but the one on the right towards the Tryp is wonderful. Don't miss the Cave nightclub. Most of the excursions are waaay overpriced: The "Caribbean Cruise" for $100 per person was a joke. I hope. Large parts of the hotel seem to be always under repair. Each time I visited there were major works projects underway

(slowly). The Fontenella a-la-carte restaurant is air-conditioned. *Info: Cayo Coco. www.blau-hotels-cuba.com/colonial/index.html; Tel. 53-33-30-1311.*

Tryp Cayo Coco $$$$

With six a-la-carte restaurants including a pizza place on the beach you

would think this is one of the better places in the area but it gets poor reviews—however they all do. The smell from the lagoon next door can be overpowering at times. Staff are constantly jockeying for tips. The beach is fairly narrow at high tide and there is a lot of activity from powered watercraft spewing fumes about and making noise. *Info: www.solmelia.com/hotels/cuba/cayo-coco/tryp-cayo-coco/home.htm; Tel. 53-33-30-1180.*

NH Krystal Laguna Villas & Resort $$$$

The resort is old and run down and is aimed at families. The pools always seem to be full of families with kids—even in the adults-only pool area. The lagoon in the middle of the resort may well have been thought of as a feature but is actually a detrimental feature. It stinks bad! The a-la-carte restaurant is sited right in the middle of it. Tipping pressure is intense. Staff expect to be tipped in dollars. I had one bartender snarlingly refuse to accept Canadian dollars as a tip. *Info: www.nh-hotels.com; Tel. 33-30-1470.*

CAYO GUILLERMO

Along the same road and within the same chain of islands, to the west of Cayo Coco, **Cayo Guillermo** is perhaps a little more upscale than Cayo Coco. The beaches are also spectacular.

Iberostar Daiquiri $$$$

This is the top-rated hotel in the Cayo Guillermo area. The grounds and gardens are lush but, in general, the place is run-down and in need of routine maintenance. The beach is very white coral sand – lovely with plenty of lounge chairs available. The pools are also nice but can be crowded—you may have to get to the pool early to score a lounge chair with umbrella.

They have a long jetty sticking out into the ocean which is good for early morning anglers. The best rooms are in the Camaguey building although some may need renovation. Newer rooms (non-smoking) are above the lobby. Try to select a room away from the disco and entertainment area.

The big "but" here, as in so many similar resorts is the terrible food. If food is an important part of your vacation, the buffets will be disappointing. Once again, it is amazing how such terrible food can be produced using what seem to be good ingredients. *Info: www.iberostar.com; Tel. 34-902-99-5555.*

Sol Cayo Guillermo $$

I generally like the Sol properties but I have to give the Sol Cayo Guillermo a medium review. They have nice white sand on the beach but it is usually littered. The pool is great—too bad about the "entertainment" blaring from loudspeakers all day. This is one of Sol's budget resorts and suffers from low occupancy. The food situation is the same here as at most of the other resorts: not so hot. The Italian a-la-carte is at least air-conditioned. The tip situation is out of control with almost every part of the buffet having a little tip plate set up for you. *Info: Cayo Guillermo. www.solmelia.com; Tel. 53-33-30-1760.*

Meliá Cayo Guillermo $$

As with all of the resorts around Cayo Guillermo, the Meliá Cayo Guillermo has a stunning beach in front of it and a nice pool – but the food is poor and the resort is run down. Air conditioning is rare in the rooms and none of the dining rooms had it when I visited. There is an elaborate animation program which makes this a good choice for families with teenagers or younger kids. *Info: Cayo Guillermo. www.solmelia.com; Tel. 53.-33-30-1680.*

CAYO SANTA MARÍA

Although in the same general area, Cayo Santa María is a separate, newer development and is reached by a causeway from the mainland to the west of the causeway to Cayo Coco and Cayo Guillermo. There are several nice beachfront resorts on the various cayos that can be reached by the new road. When I visited, several elaborate resorts were under construction and more were on the drawing boards. It is a beautiful area of low islands surrounded by clear water, reefs and shallow sand flats. On the seaward side of the islands are miles and miles of white sand beaches.

Iberostar Ensenachos $$$$

Formerly the Royal Hideaway Ensenachos, this Iberostar is built on what

is probably the nicest beach in the area. For my money this is the nicest of Cuba's all-inclusives. Rated 5 stars, the adults only resort offers more goodies than any of the others do and it's only a couple of years old. More pools (dozens) more restaurants (9), more bars (9). Their fancier suites come with 24-hour room service, stocked minibars, butler service and other perks. You can even buy a spa package for a week's worth of pampering. *Info: Cayo Ensenachos. www.iberostar.com; Tel. 53-42-35-0300.*

Meliá Buena Vista $$$$

With three restaurants, three pools and only a little over 100 rooms and suites, this is one of the smaller, quieter resorts in the area. Adults only,

there is one separate villa with its own pool, whirlpool, butler service right on the beach. The resort is a couple of miles from the others on the island. The beach is secluded and wonderful. *Info: Cayo Santa María. www.solmeliacuba.com/cuba-hotels/hotel-melia-buenavista; Tel. 42-35-0700.*

Dining Out

All-inclusive beach and buffet resorts dominate the tourism scene and there are not really many places to go for a meal outside one of the resorts. You will find a couple of beach shacks where you can get a lobster dinner for CUC 15 or so.

GUARDALAVACA

To the east, almost 100 miles of stunning but mostly unreachable beaches separate the northern cayos from Guardalavaca. Located on the mainland, Guardalavaca is one of Cuba's top beach destinations. The beaches are stunning. Many people claim the area has the prettiest water and the nicest sand anywhere in Cuba.

The resorts line up along the coast road close to the very small beach town of Guardalavaca. A wide variety of activities is available, usually booked through the resorts' tour desks.

Paradisus Río de Oro Resort & Spa $$$

Perhaps the best resort in the area, the Paradisus has 354 rooms with a few luxury suites. There are 8 restaurants with Japanese, Italian, Cuban and seafood to choose from and 5 bars. The mediocre buffet features warm food, flies and birds. The Royal Service section has its own a-la-carte restaurant which is noticeably better. Royal service rooms are definitely nicer with more luxurious furniture and larger rooms. They also have a "wellness" spa. The resort is adults only so it is good for honeymoons and romantic getaways. They offer 24-hour room service and waiter service at the pool and beach. The service is invariably extremely slow and the resort has a well-deserved reputation for rude staff and disorganization. The beach is not the nicest in Guardalavaca but still a beauty. There are tennis

courts with lights. *Info: Carretera Playa Esmeralda. www.meliacuba.com/cuba-hotels/hotel-paradisus-riodeoro/; Tel. 53-24-43-0090.*

Sol Río De Luna y Mares $$$

Big with 454 rooms, 7 restaurants, most of which are labeled "international" and 6 bars, the Sol Rio is a family resort complete with a special kids'

pool. There are tennis courts (not lighted) miniature golf (a little on the shabby side) and a rather disappointing health and fitness "spa". Bring your own tennis rackets. The ocean view rooms in the Mares section are slightly nicer but I prefer the Luna section which also has some rooms with good views. Some have large patios. Wait staff in the restaurants seem to all have been to the same rudeness school and almost demand tips. If you like cats you will love this resort. The beach is great. *Info: Carretera Playa Esmeralda. www.solmeliacuba.com; Tel. 53-24-43-0090.*

Hotel Brisas Guardalavaca $$$

The hotel is a large (450 rooms), five story building spread our around a huge pool. The beach is wonderful white sand with a little coral here and there. The water is shallow and clear. It's a great place for families with four pools, two of them set aside just for kids. They have a kids' club and a complicated animation program to keep them (and the adults) busy.

It is one of the resorts closest to the very small village of Guardalavaca where there are at least a few restaurants and a little bit of nightlife. You can easily walk back and forth to town along the beach. The resort is right on the ocean with good views from almost all of the rooms. By European

standards, the place is a little run-down and the décor is jaded. There are two buffet restaurants and two a-la-carte restaurants to choose from (seafood with lobster and Italian). The food is poor in all of them. There are several bars and two water sports centers.

Tourist Activities

The all-inclusive resorts organize almost all the touristic activities available in the area and most tend toward the cheesy side with busloads of sunburned tourists. That said there are a couple of worthwhile things to do.

The villas, which have their own pool and restaurant, are a little nicer and quieter but the views are not as good as from the upper floors in the main building. The evening entertainment and pool noise can be distracting in the main building. *Info: Calle 2, Playa. www.hotelguardalavaca.com/; Tel. 53-24-43-0218.*

BEST SHOPPING

All the resorts have gift shops selling handicrafts, rum, coffee, cigars and beachwear. Most is of appallingly low quality. I am a sucker for souvenir t-shirts and ball caps but the few available feature Fidel, Che or Sponge Bob. Oh, well. Plain brown army-style hats with a red star are usually a hit back home but you may not want to wear them into the grocery store. I always buy a couple for my friends.

CAYO COCO & CAYO GUILLERMO
El Pueblo La Estrella
Next to the Barceló the **Pueblo** is a tourist development featuring 8 restaurants: Japanese, international, Italian, seafood, steak house, Chinese, Cuban, and an Italian trattoria. There is a beer garden, ice cream parlor, honey house and a cigar house. They also have a couple of bars and a jazz café compete with the disco, bowling and billiards and a variety of snack and souvenir stores.

It is in no way, not the least bit whatsoever like a "typical" Cuban town. If you get tired of your resort you'll probably quickly get pretty tired of the Pueblo too but the shopping selection is better than in the resort gift shops.

CAYO SANTA MARÍA
There are just about zero shopping options in Cayo Santa María outside of the resorts. You may be able to find a few straw hats among the Che t-shirts in your resort's shop.

GUARDALAVACA

Guardalavaca actually has a little more shopping opportunity than most of the other beach resort areas. In the small town of Guardalavaca itself, there is a small crafts market where you can buy wood or soap stone carvings, beaded jewelry, t-shirts, leather goods, and paintings of Che.

BEST NIGHTLIFE & ENTERTAINMENT

Shows at the resorts are usually waaay overproduced but the music is almost always superb. It amazes me how great the lobby bands are especially when compared with similar offerings back in the US. The groups consist of talented, conservatory-trained musicians playing Cuban classics. I usually skip the big stage shows but hang around whenever I spot a strolling guitar player or small combo doing their thing. The music is one of the main reasons I come to Cuba and great music is not hard to find.

CAYO COCO, CAYO GUILLERMO

The **Sol Cayo Coco** has one of the best, liveliest dance clubs of the large resorts. There are very few places in the area outside the resorts to have a drink or party. However, there is a small bowling alley near the Meliá Playa Guillermo, **La Bolera**. It is a pretty sad affair but if you get too much beach, it might be worth a visit. The air-conditioning usually works.

There is a simple and dull 10pm Wednesday night cabaret show at **La Cueva de Jabalí** which is cunningly set in a small cave. There is a DJ and band most weekends. It is loud, expensive and patronized almost only by tourists. *Info: CUC 5. Tel. 33-30-1206.*

CAYO SANTA MARIA

There is a small shopping center, the Pueblo next to the Barceló that has a disco open most nights at 11pm and going on until about 3am. Cover charge is CUC 6. Other than that . . . .

GUARDALAVACA

Outside of the shows at the resorts, there are two bars and a beachside disco in the village that may be of interest.

BEST SPORTS & RECREATION

DIVING & SNORKELING

Scuba diving and snorkeling on Cuba's north coast is wonderful. Reefs are generally in good condition and loaded with fish and coral. The only problem is that most trips are aimed at beginners and snorkelers. If you are a serious diver be sure to visit the dive center at the Marina Las Brujas and arrange a private trip that does not include non-divers.

The resorts generally do quick "resort courses" in their pools and try to pack as many people on the boats as possible. Even if you are advanced open-water and have your certificate they may make you do the swimming pool session if you want to dive. The diving is good and the equipment aimed at moving the tourist cattle through the process as quickly and as profitably as possible. Do not go on a catamaran trip and expect good diving.

Cayo Coco, Cayo Guillermo
Dive sites include El Acuario, La Morena, El Perro, Las Gorgonias, Media Luna and La Jaula.

Green Moray International Dive Center
The dive center is at the Meliá and serves most of the resorts in the area. The rental equipment is ScubaPro and is in fair condition. That means that you may have small leaks from the first stage of the regulator and masks can be a bit beat up. Rental equipment goes for CUC 10 per day. They offer ACUC training. *Info: Tel. 53-33-30-1323.*

Dive sites include **La Jaula,** a 30 meter dive with large coral formations, gorgonians, sponges, large snappers, groupers, stingrays, and eagle rays. **Las Coloradas** is a 12 meter dive with small caves, and tunnels. There is a large coral boulder where you can sometimes see tarpon.

Cayo Santa Maria
Scuba diving, as organized by the resorts in the Cayo Santa Maria area involves an "initiation" in your hotel pool, equipment and instructors. You

do not have to have any prior experience. If you are not a complete klutz, it will be obvious in the pool session and you will able to go scuba diving with everyone else. Unlike proper scuba operations around the world, you do not need to have any certification to participate. Once you get past all the preliminaries, you can buy multi-dive packages. Rates are a little on the high side compared with other Caribbean destinations.

Unfortunately, diving from this marina is not at all aimed at anyone who is a serious diver. Although there are some great dive sites nearby, all the trips are to shallow areas suitable for snorkelers and rank beginners. You may be able to arrange a private trip through the staff at the marina but they refused me when I was there insisting that the snorkel trip was good for advanced divers too. Rubbish.

Guardalavaca
Fortunately, the **Eagle Ray Diving Center** on the western tip of the beach knows about proper scuba diving and takes scuba divers to 14 different sites. The reefs are great in this area and the dive operation is good.

Some of the sites are excellent without being challenging. Visibility is usually good and currents are rare.

Coral House runs to about 35' with a large coral wall and plenty of reef fish. Gorgonians and large sea fans abound.

The Crown has a small, circular coral formation with some pretty big grouper hanging about. The depth is somewhat over 100' but not too challenging.

Pretty Song, at well over 100' is a wall appealing to more advanced divers. Look for sharks, octopus and, possibly, turtles.

For black coral (don't touch!) **Fisherman** is even deeper going over 120'. There are lots of reef fish and large coral formations.

FISHING
Fishing around the cayos can be very good but it is not at the same level as fishing off Cuba's southwest coast. Deep water is just offshore but the actual Gulf Stream lies far to the west—west of Havana so, although there *is* bill-fishing, marlin and sailfish are rare. Inshore fishing for shallow water

game fish like **bonefish, snapper** and especially small **tarpon** can be good. You can arrange for a fishing charter from any of the resorts at the tour desk. You can charter an entire boat or join up with whoever is going out that day.

The boats feature trolling for tuna, snapper, and kingfish or, this is extremely unlikely, you could tangle with a marlin or other billfish. Most charters cost around CUC 300 which includes an open bar, lunch and snacks for about a half day. A full day usually goes for over CUC 500. My experience and what I hear from others tells me you actually catch something about half the time.

Cayo Coco, Cayo Guillermo
Aguas Tranquilas
The **Marina Marlin** has charters and can arrange for guides for offshore trolling and fly fishing in shallow water with prices starting at CUC 275 for a half day. Orlando Gonzalez and Dunesky Urbano are considered to be the best guides for bonefish and tarpon. *Info: Tel. 33-30-1328.*

Cayo Santa María
Tarpon fishing is particularly good in the channels and flats around Cayo Santa María. They run a little small, rarely getting over 50 lbs. but the little guys fight like hell. Marina Gaviota is the place to look for boats and guides if you don't feel like letting your resort tour desk handle it all. *Info: Tel. 42-35-0213.*

Guardalavaca
Like most of the northern resorts, there is plenty of good fishing in the area but it is simply not the same as the spectacular fishing opportunities in the southwest part of the country. There are not really large areas of sand flats to lure bonefish but there are several reasonably good tarpon holes.

Most small boats go for around CUC 180 for a half-day and CUC 300 for a full day with two anglers. Offshore trolling may produce kingfish, wahoo and a tuna if you are lucky. These boats are larger, usu-

El Baga Park Closed

The rather cheesy **El Baga Park** has recently closed but you can still stop in the area and look for **flamingos**. Most of the time they are close by but occasionally they just appear as a pink smear on the horizon.

ally take four anglers and run about CUC 250 for a half day to over CUC 500 for a full day. Both options include all the equipment you are likely to need, bait, drinks and lunch or snacks. Boats leave from the Marlin Club Las Brisas at the east end of Playa Las Brisas (where most of the resorts are). *Info: Tel. 24-43-0774.*

BIRDING

The northern cayos host a wide variety of endemic and visiting birds. Seabirds alone such as the brown pelican, laughing gull, ruddy turnstone, piping plover, and magnificent frigate bird can keep a serious birder busy for days. On the shore, look for the Cuban pee wee, Cuban bullfinch, West Indian whistling duck and of course **flamingos**. With luck you may see endemic sub-species such as Bahama mockingbird, thick-billed vireo, and mangrove cuckoo.

The now-closed **Park El Baga** is a spot where you might see flamingos. You can still wander around a little. There are still some flocks in the wild and you can see them sometimes from the causeway. They are often in the shallows on the way to Cayo Guillermo. If they are when you pass by, you can probably talk (tip) the bus driver into stopping for some quick photos. Paulino Lopez Delgado is quite a good local guide usually booked through resort activities desks. *Info: 55 CUC for a half day and 85 CUC for a full day.*

8. CAYO LARGO

HIGHLIGHTS

▲ Enjoy powdered sugar beaches

▲ Lounge about in a swim-up bar; have a cheeseburger by the pool

▲ Scuba dive or snorkel some of the world's best reefs

▲ Fish the flats for bonefish, tarpon and permit

COORDINATES

Cayo Largo is a 15.5-mile long island off Cuba's southwest coast. It is in the middle of a national marine park. There are no inhabitants on the island other than tourists and resort staff staying two weeks at a time in dormitories. Most all visitors fly into the Vilo Acuña international airport—mostly from Havana.

INTRO

Cayo Largo is a 15.5-mile long, sandy island about 20 miles off Cuba's southwest coast near Isla de La Juventud. It is one of Cuba's top **beach and buffet** destinations and has one of the nicest resorts in Cuba.

The island and the waters surrounding the island have been protected from any sort of fishing or development for over 50 years. No boats, no commercial fishing have been allowed and until recently, not even any catch-and-release sport fishing has been permitted. The ecologically sensitive region is one of the last pristine marine areas in the world.

It began its touristic life in the 1980s as a tourism destination in the same mold as Cancun in Mexico. The island has over 12 miles of the nicest white sand beaches you are likely to find anywhere in the hemisphere.

There is an international airport with direct flights from Canada, Argentina and Italy as well as several flights a day from Havana.

Cayo Largo is famous for its **beaches** and they are beauties. People seem to prefer powdered sugar, white sand on beaches and it would be hard to find any beaches anywhere whiter or more powdery than the ones at Cayo Largo. And they go on for miles.

Most of the resorts are concentrated on the beautiful **Playa Lindamar**. Beyond that are literally miles and miles of fairly deserted, classically beautiful beaches. The north side of the island is mostly swamps and mangroves.

If you walk to the far eastern end of the island, **Playa Tortuga**, you will find yourself in a deserted, beautiful wilderness. At the western end of the island, **Playa Sirena** offers what many say is the most beautiful beach in the Caribbean complete with a small bar and activities shack. There is a trolley tourists take to Playa Sirena from the resorts. There is a **nudist beach** near the Sol Cayo Largo—the only legal nudism in Cuba.

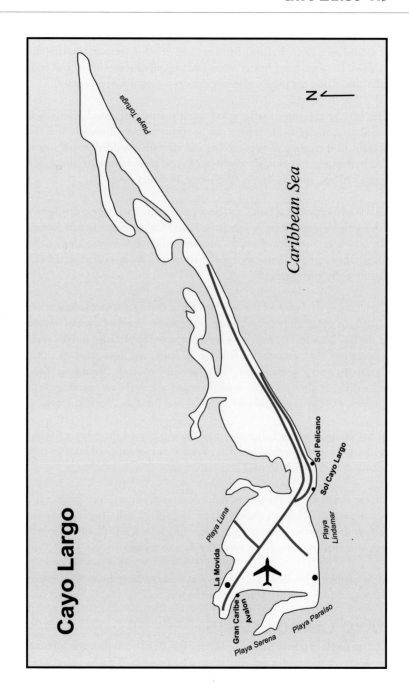

Cayo Largo is also famous for its **beach and buffet** resorts with thousands of Canadians, Brits, Italians, Russians and South Americans visiting for beaches, rum, groaning buffet tables and organized resort beach and pool activities. There are plenty of Americans enjoying the resorts as well.

The best of the resorts offer good quality air-conditioned rooms and usually reasonable food. Service can be spotty but most visitors love the bargain all-inclusive, all-**you-can-eat** and **all-you-can-drink** resort scene. The buffets are large enough so you can almost always find something that appeals to you and the drinks flow freely 24 hours a day.

This is an international beach and booze destination with great diving and fishing thrown in. There is very little actual Cuban flavor on the island. Cuban workers are brought in by boat and, when they are working on the island, they stay in dormitory-type apartments. Workers are rotated out usually every three weeks.

Cayo Largo offers some of the very best **scuba diving** and **snorkeling** in the Caribbean comparing well with top destinations like the Cayman Islands or the Bay Islands. The reefs have been protected for decades and the coral is stunning. The amount of fish life is staggering compared to other Caribbean diving destinations. Cuba carefully controls commercial fishing—there is almost none—which means the reefs are teeming with snapper, huge grouper and tiny, colorful reef fish (See *Best Activities*).

In my opinion, Cayo Largo is one of the top two or three bone **fishing** destinations in the world. Sand flats stretch for miles and hold huge schools of mudding bonefish. Permit and tarpon are common catches.

On the ocean side of the island, miles of unspoiled coral reefs protect the beaches and hold huge numbers of reef and pelagic fish. Angling over the reefs with top water plugs brings violent hits from kingfish, tuna, amberjack and vicious jacks. Great fun! (See *Best Activities*)

Most of the flights from Havana to Cayo Largo leave from the western Baracoa airport past the Marina Hemingway.

CAYO LARGO SIGHTS

The **sea turtle hatchery** is a mildly interesting, small-scale program to hatch turtles from eggs collected on the nearby beaches. The hatchlings are released shortly after emerging in a controlled manner that may ensure more of the little things reaching maturity. You'll need about 15 minutes for this.

BEST SLEEPS & EATS
Sleeps
Currently in Cayo Largo there are two hotel groups: **Gran Caribe** (5 hotels) and **Sol Meliá** (2 hotels). All hotels have direct access to the beach. The hotels are all located on the south coast of the island on the lovely **Playa Lindamar**. The resorts are 10 minutes by bus from the airport, and about 15 minutes from the village and marina. These are the best ones:

Sol Cayo Largo $$$

The Sol Club Cayo Largo is a 296-room all-inclusive resort hotel run by Meliá with a white, **powdered sugar beach** and several large pools. It is only about 5 minutes from the modern international Cayo Largo airport and also close to the marina.

This is a great place to relax after a hard day's fishing, diving or just lounging around the pool or beach. The resort is a prime vacation destination for Canadians, Europeans, Americans and South Americans. They have several pools, restaurants, nightly stage shows, bars and all the expected big resort amenities. The all-inclusive bars are not stingy with the drinks.

The best ocean view rooms (an upgrade) are on the 2nd floor of the units farthest from the lobby and closest to the sea. Even so they are a bit of a walk from the beach.

The pool is large and the bar offers reasonably good pizza but the burgers are reheated, arrive on a gigantic dry bun and come with many-times-reheated French fries. The service is good at the swim-up bar and the drinks are fine in the

usual plastic cups. The a-la-carte restaurant Las Trinas serves a decent steak and should definitely be booked as soon as you arrive. The Ranchón is not as good as the regular buffet—but the view is great.

You can always get a drink or a good cup of coffee at the bar just outside the lobby. Even if you get up at 4am there will be someone there willing to top you up. A small tip brings a smile and your generosity will be remembered the next morning at 4am.

There is a nude section on the beach and palapas where you can gaze out over the sea with a soothing tropical cocktail—all included.

If you don't let yourself get over fussy, this can be a great place to chill for a week. *Info: www.solmeliacuba.com/cuba-hotels/hotel-sol-cayolargo; Tel. 53-45-24-8260.*

Sol Pelícano $$$

Also run by Meliá the Pelícano is a reasonable second choice. Perhaps getting a bit long in the tooth, the Pelícano boasts a great beach and large saltwater pool. Towels and sheets may be a bit old and the mattresses worn and the ac can be problematic.

You can get a reasonably good chicken sandwich or BBQ at the Zun-Zun bar. You may need to ask to have your meat cooked well done. The fries can be very good The lobby bar is the place for an early morning coffee or mojito but can be very busy after 10pm when it is the only bar open.

La Yana a-la-carte is worth the wait. As in most resorts, you need to sign up for a-la-carte dining as soon as you can after your arrival. *Info: www.solmelia.com/hotels/cuba/cayo-largo/sol-pelicano/home.htm; Tel. 53-45-24-8333.*

Hotel Playa Blanca (Gran Caribe) $$

Also to be considered, for even less money than the other resorts, the 306-room Playa Blanca offers all the usual all-inclusive delights: pools, water sports and dry sports facilities, spa, sauna, daytime entertainments and evening "espectáculos". The three restaurants, buffets and a-la-cartes, are not for picky eaters. The bars are fine. An upgrade to one of their "sea view" rooms or one of their 12 suites should be considered for the views alone. You are on vacation, after all. *Info: www.playablanca.cu; Tel. 53-7-864-9177.*

Villa Marinera

A small 12-room hideaway located almost next to the marina, away from the all-inclusive resorts is the a-la-carte Villa Marinera. There is a nice pool and restaurant. Most guests are here for the diving and spend all day on or in the water. The staff is good and the drinks cold. This may be the best option for package dive trips. *Info: cubandivingcenters.com/diving-site/villa.php; Tel. 39-335-814-9111, 53-7204-7422.*

Eats

The resorts are all-inclusive and there are **almost no places outside the resorts to buy food**. Many people come specifically to enjoy the great variety of food at the resort buffets and the plentiful beer, wine, rum, mojitos and umbrella drinks. Of the resorts listed here, the best food award goes to **Sol Cayo Largo** even though it is certainly far from dining to write home to mother about.

Most people find the resort food to be fine considering what good value most of the package holidays here are. But these are not fine dining destinations. Gourmands will be happier than gourmets.

Restaurant Tip!

Tipping your waiters and waitresses at every meal will ensure your glass is always topped up. Most wait staff do not receive any tips other than what customers give them.

BEST SHOPPING

Resort gift shops usually offer basic beachwear, rum, coffee, Che t-shirts and salty or sweet snacks. There is an official cigar store near the marina where you can buy certified cigars. Other than that, shopping is pretty well limited to what you will find in the resorts' gift shops.

BEST NIGHTLIFE & ENTERTAINMENT

Most visitors spend their evenings at their resorts. All have a variety of evening music, spectaculars, talent contests and a myriad of other resort-style behavior. There is also a notorious local disco in the "village," **La Movida**, that some may find interesting.

"*Espectáculos*" are spectacular stage shows that occur almost nightly at the resorts' large concrete stages. Much of the music and dance is good and there are always a few very good musicians around, especially in the small combos that haunt lobbies and the small bars. Unless you really can't stand what is on at your own resort, I see little point in spending much effort visiting the other resorts just for their different entertainment options.

BEST SPORTS & RECREATION

All of the resorts offer the pretty much the same on-site and off-site activities that can be booked at the tour desks.

Most of the resorts are located more or less centrally on **Playa Lindamar**. **Playa Serena** and **Playa Paraíso** are to the west of the resort area and have the classic white powdered sugar like sand and a few coconut palms. This is where the resorts send you for some of the included water sports. All are beautiful beaches.

For the hardy nature lovers, a walk to the far eastern end of the island through **Playa Tortuga** takes you to a part of the island pretty much unchanged since Columbus came around.

Free trolleys run three or four times a day from the resorts to the beaches. Buses and taxis run about CUC 2 each way.

DIVING & SNORKELING

Diving here is some of the best anywhere in Cuba, or in the Caribbean for that matter. Reps from your resort can arrange for full or half-day scuba trips to nearby reefs or contact **Avalon** in advance. *Info: Avalon, www.cubandivingcenters.com; Tel. 39-335-814-9111, 53-7204-7422.*

The reefs rarely see divers and there are gigantic schools of fish, large grouper, pelagics and stunning coral formations unmatched almost anywhere else in the hemisphere (see *National Geographic* February issue, 2002). If you can bear to tear yourself away from the excellent fishing and wonderful beaches, the diving here is as good as it gets anywhere in the Caribbean.

The reefs have been protected for many years so the coral formations and quantities of fish are astounding. The marina sends out anywhere from 5 to 10 boatloads a day, mostly to the closer reefs, but the dives are still great. Often the boat will stop for a lobster lunch (extra CUCs). You can make arrangements in advance for exclusive boats to more remote locations. Catamaran or party boat trips are the way to go if you want an organized snorkeling experience. They can be expensive and usually involve more than just snorkeling.

Snorkeling is good from the beaches in front of the resorts but there is not a whole lot of coral to see. Wave action can make the visibility a little cloudy but there is usually not much rip tide action.

If you want to see a little bit more while snorkeling, the staff at Playa Sirena can arrange a small boat to take you to a very nearby section of reef for CUC 15. Also there is a bit of coral garden in front of the beach at Punta Mal Tiempo which is about halfway between Playa Sirena and the resorts. You can get the bus driver to drop you off.

FISHING

The area around the island is a protected marine fishery managed by an Italian company called **Avalon**. They have worked out a careful plan that allows them to bring in small groups of catch-and-release fly fishermen for carefully controlled fishing expeditions. The preserve is divided into six zones for environmental management purposes. Even with just 6 skiffs fishing in the entire 27,000 sq km preserve, anglers are assigned particular zones to fish in each day. The area is huge but even so the fishing zones are rotated carefully to maintain the pristine environment and keep fishing pressure to an absolute minimum.

Grand Slam

In fishing, a **Grand Slam** is when an angler catches, and releases, three of either a bonefish, tarpon, permit, or a snook all in the same day. If you catch all four you have achieved a **Super Grand Slam**. Cayo Largo is one of the most likely places in the world to achieve this piscatorial honor.

Because the area has seen virtually no negative environmental degradation over the years and since there has been no fishing in the area whatsoever for almost 50 years, the fishing is insanely great.

The huge schools of bonefish that inhabit the flats have never seen a fly, never heard the motor of a boat and are therefore uniquely unspooky and easy to catch. Anglers catch and release dozens of bonefish daily up to about 10 lbs. Snook, tarpon, permit, huge grouper and snapper are also frequent catches. The likelihood of obtaining a **grand slam** of permit, tarpon, bonefish and/or snook is probably higher in Cuba than anywhere else. *Info: Avalon, www.cubanfishingcenters.com; Tel. 39-335-814-9111, 53-7204-7422.*

BIRDING

Birdwatchers can find others of their ilk to search the eastern end of the island for a bee hummingbird or Cuban emerald hummingbird. Not uncommon are the Cuban pee wee, West Indian whistling duck, tri-colored heron, Bahama mockingbird and the piping plover.

CATAMARAN TRIPS

Catamaran trips are cool, do it. There are three boats available in the area. All the resorts book pretty much the same tours. *Lo Maximo* carries up to 30 people for large parties, *Ciprey* carries 4 to 8 people and *Azul* can take up to 10.

The all day catamaran tours include transportation to and from your resort, **open bar**, a visit to Iguana Island, plenty of snorkeling time on the reef and a beach lunch of lobster or chicken. Other little snacks and things may be included. Bring a hat and sunscreen.

9. JARDINES DE LA REINA

HIGHLIGHTS

▲ Scuba dive or snorkel unspoiled reefs

▲ Try for a Grand Slam—bonefish, permit, tarpon

▲ Enjoy the beauty of the unspoiled cays

▲ Eat lobster and a wide variety of fresh fish

COORDINATES

Los Jardines de La Reina are a 100-mile long chain of islands about 40 miles off Cuba's southwest coast. The area is a national marine park. To me, the cayos resemble what the Florida Keys must have looked like 200 years ago. There is absolutely no development of any kind on the islands.

magazine in February 2002 issue.

INTRO

Los Jardines de La Reina is a string of islands about 50 miles off Cuba's south central coast, very similar to the Florida Keys but with absolutely no one living there. This is serious *National Geographic* territory. In fact, it was featured in the

Because most of this area has been a national marine park for the last 50 years, with virtually no one fishing, diving or otherwise disturbing the environment, the fishing and diving today is unlike anything anywhere else in the hemisphere.

There are simply zillions of fish that have rarely, if ever, seen a diver or a hook. The reefs are up to 60 miles off the mainland and until recently, have rarely been visited by anyone other than the Cuban Coast Guard. I spend weeks fishing there and rarely see another boat of any type all day. This is like the Florida Keys were 200 years ago but without the pirates.

An Italian company, Avalon, has the license to take **catch and release anglers** and **divers** to the area. They maintain the 7-room hotel *Tortuga* atop a barge anchored among the islands and run 4 live aboard yachts for exploring the archipelago. Their large tender takes visitors to and from the islands from **Júcaro** on the mainland.

This is a wilderness fishing and diving destination. There is little else to do and not much in the way of beaches to walk. Most visitors come for weeklong diving or fishing packages and spend all day doing just that. They spend the evenings talking about it.

All food and most drinks are included. The huge variety and quality of the fresh seafood served here is the best I have had anywhere in Cuba. Lobster, snapper, grouper, sushi, ceviche, etc. are on the menu every night.

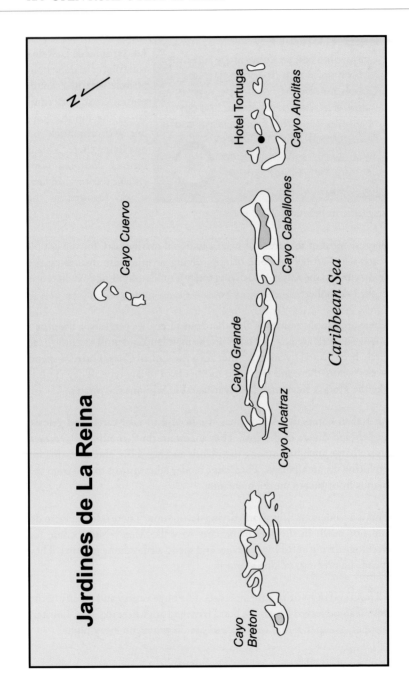

One of the most remarkable things about Los Jardines de La Reina is how quiet everything is. When your guide cuts the skiff's motor, you suddenly realize you can't hear anything. There are no sounds of airplanes, boats, jet skis, cars, nothing. As you cruise around through the cayos you also notice there are absolutely no structures of any kind—no sign of humanity is anywhere to be seen. There are no towers, radio masts, dots of buildings to mar the horizon. Nothing but sky, sand, sea and mangroves. And lots of fish.

BEST SLEEPS & EATS
Sleeps
Accommodations are good quality. All accommodations are on either the floating hotel Tortuga or four different luxury yachts. All rooms are private and air-conditioned with private baths.

Hotel Tortuga $$$
The Tortuga is a floating hotel moored in a channel between two of the cayos in the Los Jardines de La Reina island chain. Basically an enormous barge with a hotel stuck on top, there are 7 rooms upstairs accommodating 12 people and a large dining room,

kitchen and equipment area on the main deck. Staff are housed in their own nearby facilities. It's roomy with a huge staging dock along side where the skiffs tie up. There is air conditioning, hot water and you can get laundry done. This is a quite comfortable fish camp in an exotic and isolated location. *Info: Avalon, cubanfishingcenters.com/tortuga.php; Tel. 39-335-814-9111, 53-7204-7422.*

Live Aboards $$$$
Avalon offers four live aboard options for exploring angling and diving in the archipelago.

The 16-passenger **Avalon Fleet 1** is a luxury motor yacht that offers up to eight anglers and their spouses elegant staterooms, relaxation and great dining along with four skiffs and guides.

The **Halcon** is a 75' cruiser with six luxury cabins that handles 8 to 10 anglers. This mother ship anchors within a couple of minutes skiff ride to hundreds of acres of pristine flats miles and miles from any signs of civilization. These flats are loaded with bonefish.

La Reina is a 69' luxury yacht fitted out to cruise with small groups of anglers to remote parts of Jardines de La Reina. With four anglers and two skiffs and guides, the boat is set up to travel to some of the more remote areas. The boat is small enough to follow the skiffs close to the flats— usually close enough for anglers to have a nice lunch on board—maybe even a short nap.

Their fleet in this area is rounded out with the **Caballones**, which cruises with 6 to 8 anglers to remote parts of Los Jardines de La Reina along with four skiffs and guides. Based in Júcaro, the Caballones also takes exclusive groups to the untouched **South Ana Maria** area. *Info: Avalon, www.cubanfishingcenters.com; Tel. 39-335-814-9111, 53-7204-7422.*

Eats
Meals are heavy on fresh seafood including snapper prepared in interesting ways: stuffed with lobster, filleted, or whole, and of course piles of grilled lobster and various plates of ceviche and sushi. All depending on what was caught that day. Steaks and chicken are also part of every meal.

BEST SPORTS & RECREATION
Most visitors come for weeklong fishing or diving packages. The Tortuga and live-aboards are well setup for both.

DIVING & SNORKELING
There are over 120 miles of walls and reefs that have rarely or never seen a diver. The reefs are dense with fish. The water is crystal-clear. These reefs are only about 70 miles from the world-famous divers' paradise Grand Cayman Island but these Cuban reefs see only 3 or four divers a week and 10 or 20 catch and release fishermen anywhere in the 120-mile long chain of cayos. As a diver who has visited many of the prime dive locations around the world, I would rate Cuba,

No Weight Loss
You're not going to lose any weight at the fishing lodges. These are some of the few places in Cuba where you can count on the food being excellent at all times.

and Los Jardines de la Reina in particular, a 10. Right up there with the Great Barrier Reef and Palau.

Good equipment is available for rent but experienced divers know to bring your own most important equipment with you. *Info: Avalon, www.cubandivingcenters.com; Tel. 39-335-814-9111, 53-7204-7422.*

FISHING

Fly-fishing for bonefish, permit and tarpon has been bringing anglers from England, Europe, Canada and South America to enjoy these pristine fishing conditions for years. A few brave US anglers report that it is not unusual to release 20 bonefish to 12lbs. before lunch.

An easy day of fishing will typically include 10 to 20 bonefish to 12 lbs., dozens of barracuda, a shark or two, kingfish, king mackerel, 20 or 30 snapper to 40 lbs., a few grouper and tarpon to 80 lbs. and with luck, a couple of permit to 25 lbs. All catch and release, of course. Sight casting to permit, tarpon and bones on the flats, top water action over the reefs, casting to exploding bait balls with tarpon, snapper, grouper, tuna and frigate birds competing for the action, are all part of a normal day's fishing. 10 to 20 bonefish before lunch is not at all unusual.

This is **Grand Slam** and **Super Slam** territory. Bonefish are the easy part of the slam. Many anglers watching fishing shows on Saturday morning TV secretly dream of achieving a "Grand Slam". Which, for inshore fishing, means catching any three of the following four fish during the same day: tarpon, bonefish, snook or permit. If you manage to catch all four in one day, your earn an inshore Super Grand Slam.

When you are fishing in southern Cuba, Slams and grands are not dreams—they are realities that happen every week. Bonefish and tarpon are likely to be the "easy" part of achieving a slam with the wily permit being the hard piece of the puzzle to put in place. Snook are not common among the offshore cays so grand slams are fairly rare running to no more than one or two per month.

Whether you're interested in fly-fishing, spin casting or trolling you could arrive with not much more than a hat and sunglasses and do just fine but most anglers will want to bring some of their favorite kit with them. There is a well-equipped tackle store with most of the lures, flies, leaders, etc. you might need on board the Tortuga. Most people bring their own fly-fishing equipment but if you forget something or decide you need to try something different you should be okay. If particular equipment is important to you, you should give thought to bringing spares of key items. *Info: Avalon, www.cubanfishingcenters.com; Tel. 39-335-814-9111, 53-7204-7422.*

BIRDING·

Not a usual birding destination, I always enjoy seeing boobies, frigate birds and diving ducks (anhingas). Bee hummingbirds and night herons have been spotted by other visitors. If you are a non-fishing/diving spouse or if you can drag yourself away from the fishing and diving, you can arrange for one of the skiffs to take you through back channels and quiet waterways through the mangroves looking for Ferdinanda's flicker or, possibly, a Cuban pygmy-owl. Sea birds you will see include brown pelican, laughing gull, piping plover ruddy turnstone, frigate birds, boobies and neotropic cormorant

10. WESTERN CUBA

HIGHLIGHTS
▲ The remote Guanahacabibes Peninsula is a nature lover's paradise

▲ Scuba and snorkel the reefs at María La Gorda, or relax on the beach at Cayo Levisa or Villas Cabo de San Antonio

▲ Marvel at the weird *mogotes* in Viñales

▲ Tour a working farm where the best tobacco in the world is grown

COORDINATES

The western end of the island is not particularly mountainous but has some of the most interesting topography in Cuba. It is Cuba's prime tobacco growing area and has some great beaches and good fishing and diving.

INTRO

The scenic western part of the island, Pinar del Río province, produces **Cuba's best cigars**, has some of the most spectacular scenery and boasts beaches and small, remote island resorts with some of the best scuba diving in the world.

Nature lovers flock to the valley of **Viñales**, a **UNESCO World Heritage Site** famous for its picturesque pincushion hills, *mogotes,* large limestone formations dating to Jurassic times, and caves.

María La Gorda (*see photo on previous page*) is a prime scuba diving destination and the hotel can arrange for visits to the nearby **Península de Guanahacabibes** for bird watching.

On the north side of the island, **Cayo Levisa** is a popular spot for snorkelers and also has nice cabinas on a beautiful sand beach. In the evening, after the day tripping hordes leave, it is peaceful and you can walk for quite some time on the deserted beaches.

Other than on organized tours, it is difficult to get around the area without a car. If you have a week, I suggest renting a car in Havana and driving to Viñales for a night or two staying at casa particular **Casa El Porry** then moving on to **María La Gorda** for two days scuba diving. That leaves a few nights left to vegetate on the beach at **Cayo Levisa** or **Cabo de San Antonio**.

VIÑALES

To get around in the area, I like to use a local taxi driver named Carlos Madiedo Reyes, *Info: Tel. 53-311-742,* who works for Cubataxi and speaks good English, some French and Italian. He can take you to all the sights and recommend off-the-beaten-path activities, and take you to good, private restaurants so you can avoid the bland tourist fare at most places.

A **green tourist minibus** makes a loop through the valley stopping at the main caves, attractions, hotels, and in the town. For CUC 5 you can hop on and off all day.

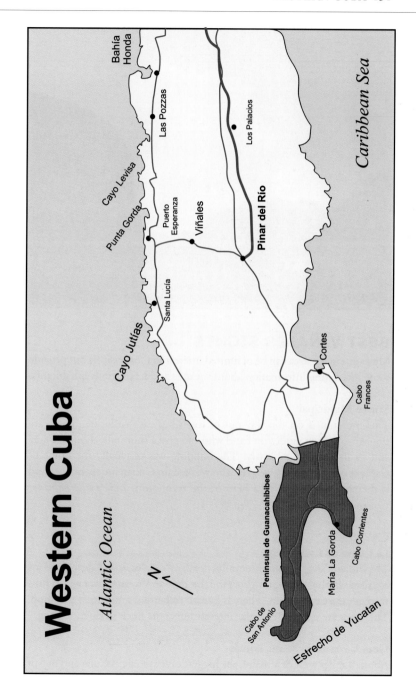

BEST VIÑALES SIGHTS

Museums in the area can be of limited interest to most visitors but provide some interesting information about the area and its previous inhabitants.

Museo Municipal

This museum is on the way out of town but easy to locate. There are English-speaking guides on hand who can give a short talk about the area and its development history. The building was originally the home of Captain Adela Azcuy, a woman who worked for Cuban independence and is therefore somewhat of a hero of the revolution. *Info: Calle Salvador Cisneros 115. Tel. 53-082-79-3395.*

CAVES

La Cueva de Los Indios

The Indian Caves, about three miles north of Viñales, is well developed for tourism offering lights and a boat tour on the San Vicente River which runs through the cave system. There is a small restaurant and cheesy gift shop. The caves are not of particular interest but tours flock to them anyway.

Gran Caverna de Santo Tomás

About 9 miles west of Viñales, the biggest cave system in Cuba and one of the largest in Latin America, Santo Tomas is for serious cavers and has 32 miles of galleries on eight levels. All tours are with guides and visitors must wear the provided helmets with headlights. The tours last around two hours and cost CUC 5. You must wear shoes—no sandals. The cave tour is one of the best things to do in the Viñales area, in my opinion running a close second to **visiting the tobacco farms** (*see photo below*)—which you should arrange with your hotel.

BEST SLEEPS & EATS
Sleeps

Viñales is one of the busier tourist areas in Cuba but has only two main hotels, **La Ermita** which has a nice pool and rather average food and **Jazmines** which has a pool and poor food. Both have stunning views of the mogotes in the countryside. They can fill up fast so you should reserve in advance rather than hope to just walk in. Please take my advice and skip these hotels in favor of staying in a casa particular, privately run B&B.

Viñales happens to have some of the nicest casa particulars in Cuba so you should have no trouble finding comfortable lodging and good food. They cost less than a third of the hotels rates and you can expect wonderful meals and a friendly atmosphere.

La Ermita $$$$

The aging Ermita has a nice pool and great views over Viñales valley. Other than that, the rooms are small and run-down, the buffet is on the poor side,

even for Cuba, and the staff speaks little English and has almost no tourism information available. If you bring a car, watch out for their car wash scam—your car gets washed overnight without your asking—a nice service included at some upscale hotels in the world but the attendant here acts extremely put out when you refuse to pay. Tough luck for him.

The views from the pool are great but the bar blasts pop reggaeton at ear-splitting level and staff seems puzzled by requests to turn it down. *Info: Carretera de La Ermita km.1 1/2. www.hotel-la-ermita-cuba.com.*

Los Jazmines $$

Great *mogote* views. Fairly big with 78 rooms and villas but, although newer than the Ermita, it is still very basic and in bad need of routine maintenance. The pool is nice but often crowded with staff members and their families. Service and food are fairly typical for Cuba—not so hot. There is not much to do in the evening as the downstairs bar is rather drab and serves as the

hangout for local taxi drivers. The rooftop bar is better. There is a bit of an evening show with dancers and fire-eaters. The location is far from a

town of any sort. There is an unbelievable assortment of mangy dogs and cats constantly on the prowl for handouts. *Info: Carretera de Viñales km. 25.*

Villa Tito y Janet $$

A fairly new casa particular only a couple of blocks from the main street, Villa Tito y Janet is run by a small family. The son speaks quite good

English and the food and facilities are good. *Info: Calle Adela Azcuy #18; Tel. 48-793-199.*

Casa El Porry $$
This casa particular backs onto quiet farmland and has good views from the rooftop lounge area. The owners do not speak much English but offer clean, air-conditioned rooms with a private bath. *Info: Calle Salvador Cisnero; Tel. 53-311-744.*

Casa Ony y Luis $$
At the edge of town with a good view of the *mogotes*, this casa has comfortable beds, private rooms with private bath and a sitting area. Complementary fruit juices are wonderful. The host Luis speaks good English and is friendly and outgoing without going overboard. Drinks and meals are very well done with a decent wine. *Info: Calle Cooperativa Manuel Fajardo.*

Eats
The only good places to eat in Viñales are in the *casas particulars*, privately run B&Bs, where you can usually expect great meals and a friendly atmosphere. Some of the casas will serve wonderful meals. Ask in advance if possible. Food in this area as in most of Cuba can be hit or miss. Hotels and government run restaurants are usually poor choices.

Paladar Casa Don Tomas $$
Probably the most popular place to eat in Viñales, they specialize in a paella-like dish with seafood over rice. The food is well above what you usually find in Cuba but still tends to be bland and overcooked. They have nice stews served in earthenware bowls. Drinks are nice with their specialty, a *Trapiche*, made with rum, pineapple juice, and honey with a sugar cane swizzle stick. Nice. The historic building is a national monument oozing with atmosphere and interesting architectural details. The best tables are on the two patios. *Info: Salvador Cisneros #140; Tel. 48-893-6300.*

Villa Pupi y Norma $$
This casa particular can cook up a great dinner or lunch if you ask in advance. They have good food and are located on a quiet street. Their seafood dinners are very good with snapper or lobster. *Info: Calle Camillo Cienfuegos # 8.*

Casa Colonial Mercedes $$
Friendly service, good food, ask in advance if possible. The colonial style

building has a nice patio for lunch or dinner. Their portions of fruit, chicken and seafood are *very* large. *Info: Rafael Trejo # 2.*

BEST SHOPPING

As in most of Cuba, shopping opportunities are rather slim. You can purchase cigars right at the farms in the Viñales area but, since these are not official Cuban cigar stores, you may have problems when you try to leave the country with them.

María La Gorda and the cayos to the north offer a few gaudy gift shop handicrafts and the usual hats and t-shirts featuring Che.

BEST NIGHTLIFE & ENTERTAINMENT

Although this is one of the more popular parts of the country for tourism, there is little to no nightlife aside from what is provided in hotels and restaurants, which is almost always of poor quality. There simply are not many places to go out at night.

Cueva de San Miguel, just outside Viñales, turns into a tourist-trap nightclub in the evenings. Unless you are really hard up for nighttime activity, skip this one and go to bed early.

BEST SPORTS & RECREATION

A bird-watching trail begins at the **El Ranchón restaurant** near the Cuevas del Indio and leads about two miles through nearby farms and forest areas. You should look for the Cuban trogon, tody, Cuban solitaire (mockingbird), hummingbirds and a passerine in the pine forests. The **Casa de Caridad Botanical Garden**s is also a good place for birding.

In the western end of the island it is easy to spot the endemic Cuban solitaire and a near endemic: olive-capped warbler. The caves around Viñales are home not just to zillions of bats but also large colonies of cave swallows.

There are many different microclimates in western Cuba. You may see some of the following birds: red-legged honeycreeper, greater Antillean grackle, Cuban grassquit, Cuban trogon, western spindalis, Antillean palm swift, or a giant kingbird. The **Guanahacabibes Peninsula** is considered prime birding territory.

MARÍA LA GORDA

María La Gorda features a large diving operation with usually two boats taking divers to over 50 well-documented dive sites. Walls and wrecks are the main attractions. Some of the dive sites are very close to the marina and the most remote are only about an hour away.

If you want to spend several days in the area, have a long talk with the dive master when you arrive to be sure you arrange dives to several locations. The captains' tendency is to simply drive the boat to one or two of the closest sites, shove everyone overboard and wait for them to come back. You may have to be insistent or arrange for a private boat to get to some of the more interesting sites. Although the boats are not overlarge, there is still a cattle boat mentality.

BEST SLEEPS & EATS
Sleeps
Villa Cabo San Antonio $$

Waaay out at the most western tip of Cuba, the Cabo San Antonio is isolated, quiet and comes with lots of nature. Wild cows, pigs, iguanas roam about. The beach is not like the white sand cayo beaches and the water can be rough but is still wonderful. It is not a manicured beach like in front of the big resorts—it is a "natural" beach as befits its UNESCO status. Expect bugs. The snorkeling is great. Turtles nest in May.

The "resort" is very basic. There is nothing to buy and you need to pay cash for all meals. The food is average by Cuban standards. It is worth it to pay the extra CUC 5 to get a room with an ocean view. The hotel is located in an UNESCO protected biosphere. There are 16 rooms in 8 wooden cabins with double beds and air-conditioning.

The road from María La Gorda is long and rough in places but well worth the effort. There are no organized activities of any sort. Read, swim, walk, talk is the whole deal. There is a simple marina that offers fishing trips. The place dates from 2006 so is still in good condition. *Info: cabo de San Antonio. www.villacabosanantonio.com; Tel. 53-48-75-0118.*

Villa María La Gorda Gaviota $$

The old part of the lodge is unbelievably rundown with broken windows, busted plumbing, crumbling walls and doors that don't quite close. They are on the sand under the palm trees so there is at least a bit of character. The newer units are set back from the beach with little view.

There are two restaurants but one is closed during low season. The buffet is on the poor side. One night I was there they had nothing but dried out chicken, some rolls and shredded cabbage. Really. That was dinner. I suggest bringing a few things to eat with you. There is almost nothing to buy in the area and it is a long way to any village or town. There are dozens of cats wanting to join you for your meal. Bring your own wine. *Info: Península de Guanahacabibes, Sandino.*

Eats

There are no real choices outside of the hotels.

BEST SPORTS & RECREATION

Diving and snorkeling at María La Gorda or Cayo Levisa is excellent. Divers from around the world come for wall and wreck dives and for the well-preserved coral formations. Dive operations in both locations are good with equipment in reasonable condition and well trained, although not necessarily enthusiastic dive masters.

For divers, this is one of the better places to dive in Cuba. There are around 50 formal dive sites within an hour of the marina. Whale sharks come around in October and November and the reefs are in good condition.

There is **fishing** at the marina but almost no equipment is available. There are some bonefish on the flats but most fishing will be trolling just offshore. Near María La Gorda, the **Guanahacabibes Peninsula** is one of Cuba's **top birding areas** and probably the best spot for seeing the world's smallest bird: the bee hummingbird. Cuba's national bird, the Cuban Trogon is easy to find there as well as the Cuban tody. Sea birds and wading birds are very common.

CAYO LEVISA

Cayo Levisa is a small island about a mile offshore reachable from the mainland by ferry. There is one small resort on the island and not much to do besides walk on the beach or go snorkeling. The island is on a list of day trips for tourists visiting Viñales. Be sure you don't miss the last ferry to the island at 6pm or you will have to find other accommodations—perhaps back in Viñales or Havana.

BEST SLEEPS & EATS
Sleeps
Hotel Cayo Levisa $$$
The older cabins on the beach are a little run down but are the best for beach views. The newer rooms are a little better but try to book #15 – 20. 20 has a nice view. There is seriously nothing to do here besides walk on the beach and go diving. The lounge is a little old but there is a nice bar. Food can be iffy. The buffet is standard Cuban so you need to arrive early and try to get something fresh.

The shop sells rum and a few basics. I absolutely love the place as do most nature lovers. This is not a fancy beach destination with activities—you make your own fun. They have AC and TV. The staff can be quite rude and inattentive. Day-trippers

arrive at 10:30 and can clog up the facilities. The diving is mostly geared to snorkelers and you have to talk hard and fast to get to the better dive sites. *Info: www.hotelescubanacan.com; Tel. 03-75-6507.*

Eats
There are no real choices outside of the hotel.

BEST SPORTS & RECREATION
Cayo Levisa is small with only one smallish resort which specializes in taking busloads of day-trippers on shallow-water snorkeling trips. Scuba diving is excellent however with large, well-developed reef systems. Because the dive shop specializes in mass-tourism snorkeling, it is a little difficult to arrange scuba-specific trips to the deeper reefs.

When I went I found the dive master to be very sympathetic and agreed to set up smaller, scuba-only trips for me and my companions. Each time though, when we were ready for our scuba trip, apologies were made and we had to go to a shallow reef with 40 or so snorkelers. We simply refused to go at all on the third day.

Interestingly, whenever we went out on the dive boat, a fully uniformed soldier complete with machine gun accompanied us while his companion watched the whole trip from the shore through binoculars. At this point on the island, it is a very short hop to Key West so the boats are carefully monitored to avoid any detours to freedom. Diving is expensive at CUC 55 per dive. The five-dive package is difficult to take advantage of unless you are there for several days or will be happy to dive the same snorkeling site every day.

FISHING
Fishing is not high on the list of tourist activities in western Cuba although, if you can arrange for a boat, it can be excellent. Bring your own tackle or expect to be trolling with a hand line and chicken scraps for bait.

BIRDING
Cayo Levisa is designated a refuge for pelicans and other large birds which are certainly in evidence. There is not much in the way of trails or walks other than along the beach but wading birds are easy to view and I have

heard reports of sightings of the bee hummingbird although I saw none when I was there. There are no guides of any sort available through the hotel.

11. PRACTICAL MATTERS

GETTING TO CUBA
AIRPORTS/ARRIVALS

All of the international flights arrive at Havana's **José Martí International Airport**. It's old and crummy, a Soviet-style concrete monstrosity with no glitterati-type duty free shops. There are five terminals. There is no shuttle or transit service between terminals and it is much too far to walk. You'll have to take a cab and the cabbies seem puzzled why anyone would want to change terminals.

Flights within Cuba generally leave from one of the secondary terminals at José Martí International Airport or from the airport just outside of Havana to the west: **Aeropuerto Baracao.**

Dozens of security types pack the international arrivals terminal grilling anyone who appears slightly suspicious, has long hair or is in any other way out of the ordinary. Drug-sniffing dogs are ubiquitous so leave your stash at home.

Take care when you fill out the little arrivals forms. In Cuba they take these very seriously and the customs officials read every word and question you about your entries. Do not list anything as your occupation that may cause concern. Cuba does not like independent writers, filmmakers, political activists or humanitarian types. Be a truck driver instead. Getting upset about this will only make things worse.

Most flights from North America and Europe arrive in the afternoon. Taxis to the city cost from $20 to $25.

Flights to Cuba tend to funnel through Mexico City, Miami, Panama, Cancun, Nassau, London and Madrid.

Departures

Check in is usually fairly efficient but be sure to keep CUC 25 per person handy for airport departure tax. No airlines include the fee and it must be paid in CUCs after check in. No exceptions.

Like almost all buildings in Cuba, the airport buildings are built entirely of concrete so the acoustics are challenging. Garbled announcements over the ultra-loud PA system are unintelligible. Keep an eye on your departure gate and ask a flight attendant if you think something important may have been announced.

Sadly, the departure area of the airport has almost nothing to eat other than the usual, low quality spam sandwiches and cookies. I saw a couple of sad looking apples on my last trip. The coffee is good but be sure you eat something before you get there.

Airport shopping offers the usual gaudy Che t-shirts and crummy hats. There is a decent selection of coffee, cigars and rum but the prices are higher than I see in stores in town.

Leaving the country with cigars not purchased at an official state cigar store is against the law. Attempting to do so is smuggling and may result in you being detained at the airport.

CRUISES THAT VISIT CUBA

Almost no cruise lines target Cuba although a couple of companies have announced plans to start service.

Tropicana Cruises LTD

Tropicana has recently inaugurated their cruise around the island. It departs from Havana and stops off in Isla de la Juventud (Isle of Youth),

Trinidad, Cienfuegos, Ocho Rios in Jamaica, Santiago de Cuba and Cayo Saetia. *Info: 9-10 Johnston Road, Woodford Green, Essex, IG8 0XA, UK. www.tropicanacruises.com; Tel. 44-208-498-9410.*

Fred Olsen Cruise Lines
Leaves from ports such as Montego Bay and Southampton with stops in Havana and Santiago de Cuba. They stop briefly in Ocho Rios, Jamaica. *Info: Fred. Olsen House, White House Road, Ipswich, Suffolk, IP1 5LL, www.fredolsencruises.com; Tel. 44-1473-74-2424.*

GETTING AROUND CUBA
BY AIR
Flights within Cuba are relatively expensive and service levels are lower than in most countries. Food and beverage service is spotty but when it does occur usually involves spam sandwiches, over-sweet cookies and strange Tang-like beverages. Waiting rooms are primitive concrete affairs often with reggaeton blaring from the TV driving travelers into the parking lot to wait for flights.

Some of the planes are a little on the creaky side and are definitely not up to high US standards, but accidents are rare. I have been in several where I could see light around the edges of the door and feel a draft after taking off. This was fine since the AC didn't work very well anyway. This is part of why they call it "adventure travel."

BY CAR
Driving yourself around the country provides flexibility and convenience. Main roads are generally pretty poor but roads in isolated areas can be

amazingly bad. At least there is not much traffic and Cuban drivers are reasonably attentive. If you rent a small, compact sedan, you will probably find yourself bottoming out in large, pond-sized mud puddles and cow-sized potholes. At these times simply grit your teeth and hope you don't puncture the oil pan. Driving anywhere in the country at night is simply not wise.

Road signs are rare. Signs identifying small villages or large towns are just about nonexistent. At some rural crossroads, you may see a sign far down one branch. Drive down and look at it, as it may have relevant information. Realize that many locals standing by the side of the road have no more idea how to get to the next village than you do. It is best to ask other drivers, cops or truck drivers for directions. Gas station attendants are another possible source for road information. Ask more than one person and ask often. Conflicting directions are part of the adventure. To foil possible Yankee invaders, Cuban maps show non-existent roads and do not show some existing roads. This can be a problem.

Car Rental

There are plenty of car rental offices but not plenty of rental cars. Most of the large hotels have agency offices and are your best bet. There are several government-run agencies with little difference between them. Prices, car types and availability vary from office to office so, if your Spanish is up to it, you could call around to find the best deal.

Choices of car types are not good. You pretty much have to take what they offer you. Check carefully for damages before leaving the rental office. Rates are higher than you may be used to paying in the US averaging around CUC 80 per day with unlimited mileage.

The different agencies usually only rent the cars that happen to be in their parking lot. One branch office across town may have cars available but the other branch offices won't know it and the office you are dealing with may tell you they have no cars available. Try another office.

You may be able to hire a private driver with car for almost the same amount as a straight-ahead rental car. See below.

Cubacar
Ave 5ta y 84, Miramar. www.cubacar.cubanacan.cu/english/default1.htm; Tel. 53-7-24 2718.

Havanautos
Ave 5ta y 84, Miramar. www.havanautos.cu; Tel. 53-7-24 2718.

Via Rent a Car
Ave del Puerto. Edificio La Marina. 3er piso, Habana Vieja. www.gaviota.cubaweb.cu/espannol/rentcar/index.php; Tel. 53-7-66-6777.

Panautos
Calle Línea y Malecón, Vedado. www.cuba.cu/turismo/panatrans/panautos.htm; Tel. 53-55-3255.

Private Drivers
The best way to enjoy a short stay in Havana and other parts of Cuba is to hire an English-speaking driver. You can hire almost any cab in town for $10 an hour, but most drivers speak only fair English, if any. For a very professional Spanish-speaking driver, I suggest you contact Jorge to guide you around town. *Info: jorgeguide2004@yahoo.es.* The charge is around $12 an hour but it's worth it.

Rafael Lorenzo
Speaks very good English and is experienced in escorting travelers all over the island. He is sophisticated, well dressed, in his mid-thirties and speaks several languages (including English). He knows the music scene in Havana and can help you get great tables at the best music places. He can take you to meet young Cuban artists and can secure invites to private parties with actors and directors. *Info: rafaellorenzo22@yahoo.com; Tel. 05-796-7584, 05-281 8462.*

Gran Car
You can hire one of those cool 1950s American cars with driver to drive you around in major cities. They charge CUC 15 per hour but you can bargain for longer periods. *Info: www.cuba.cu/turismo/panatrans/grancar.htm; Tel. 81-7931.*

BY TAXI
There are several types of taxis tourists can take in Cuba. None are

particularly cheap but, especially in Havana, you'll need to take them from time to time.

Almost all taxis are supposedly under the umbrella of **Cubataxi** but many still have the old signs and charge the old prices. Whether or not the taxi you get into has a meter, ask for the price before you get in. Look for a "1" on the meter for daytime rates and a "4" at night.

The bright yellow, egg-looking jobs or "**coco taxis**" are for tourists only and get you from place to place in Havana for a usually reasonable fare.

The yellow **Cubataxis** are usually the cheapest but are not allowed to pick up in front of tourist hotels. You can usually find them parked a short distance away.

Usually **Panataxi** will be the cheapest. **Turistaxi**, **Transgaviota** and **Taxi OK** are the most expensive. Some of the yellow taxis are for Cubans only and simply will not stop for tourists no matter how desperate you seem. **Grancar** taxis are old US cars with a small sign on the side. They are usually high-priced running to over CUC 30 per hour. You can find them in front of the major hotels like the Nacional or the Parque. Around the Parque Central you can find dozens of the old US cars offering their services— sometimes informally.

Horse drawn carriages cost around CUC 30 per hour and can be an entertaining way to enjoy the Malecón.

Bicitaxis are really for Cubans only but they will often take tourists and hope the cops don't catch them. They usually go for about CUC 1.

Almendrones/Colectivos are shared taxis, usually old US cars with little red and white *taxi* signs on the right side. They go on a fixed route from one end of town to the other. You can hop in and out. Almendrones start their route at Parque Central at the corner of Prado and Neptuno and go on a route towards Miramar. It costs CUP 20 to go all the way to Miramar and CUP 10 to go to Vedado. What a deal!

BY BUS
Buses are a good way to get around the country. There are several types of buses offering distinct levels of comfort. *Gua-gua* is the slang for bus. You may see a few of the old-style *camelos*, broken back looking contraptions hooked on to old tractor trailers packed, packed, packed with people. You will probably want to avoid these just for comfort's sake but there are other good options.

Regular city buses, marked for their routes M1–M7 run regular routes and are usually packed. Expect to stand. They cost CUP 5 – pay when you get in.

Viazul is an excellent way to get around the country with modern, air-conditioned buses with comfortable seats. The ac can get extremely cold so bring a sweater. The DVDs advertised as a "feature" on these buses are often turned up to earsplitting level and feature kung fu-type action films and Celine Dion videos. You have been warned. Book the day before you plan to travel. *Info: 26th Ave. y Zoológico, Nuevo Vedado. Tel. 81-1413.*

Astro buses run all over the island and are cheaper than Viazul without seats reserved for foreigners. Tourists pay in CUCs and locals pay in CUPs. *Info: Avenida de La Indepencia y Calle 19 de Mayo. Tel. 53-7-870-9401.*

BY TRAIN
Although you will see some old steam trains still working hauling sugar cane around, there is really just one train line in Cuba. It runs from Havana to the far end of the island stopping in major towns and is extremely slow, unreliable and uncomfortable. It is not a fast way to travel. The trip to Santiago takes about 13 hours.

Service and schedules are uncertain. Food onboard is dire. The nasty bathrooms are almost comical in their lack of doors, toilet seats and toilet paper.

Train Station
Leave Cuban trains to hard-core train buffs. They run from Havana to Guantanamo with many stops, are old, slow, often crowded and notoriously many hours or even days late. *Info: Avenida de Bélgica. Tel. 537-862-1920.*

BASIC INFORMATION
BANKING & CHANGING MONEY

Change your foreign currency for convertible pesos, CUCs, pronounced *"kooks"* at one of the official **CADECAs**. These change bureaus are located in hotels, airports and other spots tourists might visit. Hotel front desks also offer currency exchange but possibly at a higher rate. Some airports have a CADECA only in the departure hall so you may need to walk around to get some cash.

ATMs?

Although some ATMs will accept VISA, it would be best not to plan on using ATMs no matter where your cards are issued. There are not all that many machines available anyway. Cards affiliated with Cirrus or Maestro networks are unusable in Cuba. Most banks and CADECAs will give VISA or MasterCard cash advances if the cards have no US affiliation.

Rates vary from CADECA to CADECA but usually not by very much. The airport rates are not always worse than CADECAs in town. Scrutinize you receipt, *factura*, carefully before leaving. The government charges a 10% fee for changing US dollars. Exchange rates are set by the government rather than by the international currency markets. Currently, after the 10% fee, one CUC is worth roughly US$ 1.25 or slightly more. Your US dollar does not go very far in Cuba.

US credit cards are absolutely not accepted in Cuba. Capital One, American Express, Egg and MBNA cards will not work in Cuba. Unless your cards are issued by a non-US bank, bring enough cash for your whole trip. With VISA and MasterCard from Europe or Canada, with none of the USA affiliations mentioned, you should be able to draw funds from banks ATMs or CADECAs.

Be aware that the currency situation in Cuba changes from time to time. Currently, there are two official Cuban currencies: **Cuban Pesos**, CUP and **Convertible Peso** or "CUCs" as they are called. The rate is 24 CUP to 1 CUC. Neither CUPs nor CUCs are changeable or of any use outside

of Cuba. Tourists are expected to change their international currency into CUCs for use on the island.

Cubans' salaries are paid in CUPs which they use to purchase rum, pizza, coffee, tobacco, ice cream, tickets to sporting events and entertainment venues, some food items, electricity, water and can be used in Peso bars and restaurants. CUCs are needed for everything else. Cubans can only get hard currency from foreigners or from family members who send it from overseas.

Tourists are expected to convert their US dollars, Euros or GBP for CUCs. CUCs are accepted almost everywhere. Almost anything the average visitor will want to spend money on is priced in CUCs.

BOOKING TOURS & ACTIVITIES
Within Cuba, there are several government-run tour agencies:
• **Cubanacán**, *Tel. 537-204-4756*
• **Cubatur**, *Tel. 537-836-4155*
• **Gaviota**, *Tel. 537-209-4528*
• **Paradiso**, *Tel. 537-832-9538*

BUSINESS HOURS
Shops and offices are usually open from 9am to 5pm. Tourism businesses

may open earlier and stay open into the evening. Be prepared for unexpected closures. Employees may decide to take longer than usual lunches or not come back from lunch at all.

CLIMATE & WEATHER
Cuba's climate is temperate to semitropical. Mountain regions can get chilly. Cuba's average minimum temperature is 70° and the maximum is 81° with an average of 77°. Not bad. Trade winds and ocean breezes make for great seaside weather.

The rainy season is from May to October and usually features occasional afternoon tropical squalls. Hurricanes may batter the island from August through December.

CONSULATES & EMBASSIES
Havana has embassies and consulates from most countries except for the US.

The **United States Special Interest Section** (under the protection of the Swiss Embassy) is only to be approached in absolute emergencies.

Havana Temp. Chart

January	69°
February	70°
March	72°
April	76°
May	78°
June	79°
July	80°
August	80°
September	79°
October	79°
November	74°
December	71°

Although I have no personal experience with the situation, I have been told by people who unfortunately found themselves in difficult situations that they will help US citizens who have lost passports/money with little or no hassle about their possibly illegal status in Cuba.

Canadian Embassy
Info: Calle 30 No. 518, Miramar. www.canadainternational.gc.ca; Tel. 7-204-2516.

British Embassy
Info: Calle 34 no. 702 e/ 7ma y 17, Miramar. www.ukincuba.fco.gov.uk/en; Tel. 7-214-2200.

United States Special Interest Section
Associated with the Swiss Embassy. *Info: Calzada between L & M Streets, Vedado. www.havana.usint.gov; Tel. 7-833-3551.*

CUSTOMS INFORMATION
Visitors to Cuba should expect a more thorough inspection than they receive in most countries. Customs inspectors carefully examine the immigration cards you fill out on the plane and may ask you detailed questions about your travel plans in Cuba and your general travel history. Arriving visitors may bring cell phones, iPods, and most advanced electronic gadgets into the country with no problem. Tourists may not bring GPS devices, satellite phones or anything even slightly resembling pornography. A variety of magazines and books are also prohibited.

There is a $20 tourist visa that must be purchased by all visitors. It is usually sold when you purchase your air ticket.

Departure is fairly straightforward with the usual baggage inspection procedures as in any international airport. There is a CUC 25 airport fee payable in CUCs in the ticketing hall.

Visitors may take 23 cigars and 1.14 liters of alcohol, which is about two regular bottles, with no problem.

Be aware that the only cigars that may be legally taken out of the country are cigars purchased in an official government cigar store. Any other cigars, no matter how you came by them, even if they were given to you or if you made them yourself cannot be taken out of the country. Carrying street purchased cigars in your carryon baggage is smuggling and may be punished.

Artwork, artifacts and various artisanal items need to have a stamp from the National Registry of Cultural Objects before you can take them with you. Watch for this when you purchase art. Books over 50 years old may not be taken out of the country.

ELECTRICITY
Electric current and fixtures in Cuba are pretty much the same as in the US but with the addition of European-style round pin outlets combined in the same outlet. Many times you will see 220 outlets of exactly the same type side by side with the 110 sort. Sometimes they are not labeled. Sometimes you will fry your electronic device by accident. Plugs are usually two-prong and not grounded. You may want to bring along a three prong-to two prong adaptor or just twist of the ground prong off whatever appliance you simply must use.

Remote lodges may run on generators or solar power. Some may turn the power off at night. This means you may not be able to run your laptop or hairdryer whenever you like. Blackouts, *apagones*, are common in all parts of the country and can last for several hours. This is just part of life in Cuba. Enjoy.

EMERGENCIES & SAFETY

If you have serious problems and your hotel front desk is unable to help, you can call the police yourself although English-speaking police officers are rare.

Police Department
Tel. 106

Fire Department
Tel. 105

Crime

Downtown Havana seems to have at least one cop standing on every corner. Roadside motorcycle police vigorously enforce traffic laws. They will stop you if they see you are not wearing seat belts. Unlike in the rest of Latin America, Cuban drivers go slow, come to complete stops at lights and stop signs, always wear their seat belts and usually drive very slowly and carefully. You rarely see any vehicles with a broken headlight or taillight—the cops hand out serious fines and jail time to offenders.

Because of the heavy police presence, crime seems to be much less in Cuba than in many countries. Pickpockets and muggings are relatively rare but you need to be very careful in crowds and clubs. Walking around town late at night is not advised.

The type of crime most tourists will experience is being ripped off, overcharging in bars, restaurants, hotels—almost any financial transaction. All these places are government run and employees receive shockingly low salaries. Most tips you see listed on your receipt do not go to your server but to the government.

In many restaurants and bars you will notice that servers rarely actually ring anything up on the cash register—they are pocketing as much as they think they can get away with. Demand a bill, *factura*, and check it carefully before handing over your money. You will very often find discrepancies. Be firm—they are not going to call the cops on you if you refuse to be ripped off.

HEALTH
You do not need any special inoculations or shots before visiting Cuba. Malaria and yellow fever are pretty much things of the past. Drinking water from the tap is not a good idea in most places. Hotels offer guests bottled water (*agua mineral* or *agua pura*) in their rooms for a small charge. Use condoms, dummy. AIDS, known internationally as SIDA, certainly exists in Cuba, as do other loathsome venereal diseases.

In the large, all-inclusive resorts, be prepared to pay CUC 25–40 for a doctor visit plus the cost of medication. Hospitals for foreigners are slightly better than most but still are seriously under-equipped. Common medicines and medical supplies are in short supply. Expect to pay serious money for anything you have done in a Cuban hospital.

Although there is still some medical tourism to Cuba, the famous Cuban health system is slowly sinking into developing world status and fewer people come for treatment

International Drug Stores
There are a couple of drug stores where you may be able to find medicines when you need them but they are very poorly stocked and expensive.

Farmacia Internacional Miramar
Ave. 41 esquina a 20, Miramar, Havana, Tel. 53-7-204-4350

Clínica Central Cira García
This is the hospital most tourists will be sent to. There are many English-speaking staff and it is clean and professional. *Info: Calle 20 #4101 Miramar. Tel. 53-7-204-4300.*

Hotel Habana Libre
Calle L e/ 23 y 25, Vedado, Havana, Tel. 53-7-55-4593

HOLIDAYS & CELEBRATIONS
Many of the special days you would expect to celebrate, like Christmas, Easter or Halloween simply do not happen in Cuba. Many of their holidays have a revolutionary theme.

January
- Liberation Day January 1.
- José Martí's birthday January 28.

February
- Feria Internacional del Libro is a month-long book fair.
- Havana Jazz Festival.

March
- Fiesta de Toronja celebrating citrus fruits is held on the Isle of Youth.

April
- Havana hosts a world-famous International Film Festival.
- There is a biennial Humor Festival centered on San Antonio de los Baños near Havana.

May
- May 1 sees Labor Day celebrations in the Plaza de la Revolución. This is where Fidel used to give four and five hour-long speeches.
- Independence Day May 20.
- International Hemingway Fishing Tournament is held at the end of the month at the Marina Hemingway just outside Havana.

June
- Jornada Cucalambreana near Las Tunas is a music festival celebrating a country style of music.
- Fiestas Sanjuaneras in Trinidad celebrates the Cuban cowboy lifestyle.

July
- The 26th is the Anniversary of the Revolution, Día de La Rebeldía Nacional, and a celebration in memory of Fidel's failed attack on the Moncada Barracks in Santiago. Santiago is famous for one of the most elaborate Carnival celebrations in the Caribbean.

August
- Festival Internacional Havana Hip-Hop celebrates, you guessed it, hip-hop in all its Cuban glory.

September
• Probably the best of Cuba's musical celebrations, Festival Internacional de Música de Benny More is held every year in Santa Isabel de Las Lajas. The king of Cuban music, Benny More is revered all over the island and could be favorably compared to Duke Ellington for his influence on the Cuban sound.

October
• Festival International De Ballet de La Habana is held on even-numbered years and features popular and classical performances by the national ballet and guest dancers from around the world.

November
• Fiestas de Los Bandas Rojas y Azul in Ciego de Avila features dance and music competitions between two halves of the town.
• Marabana is Havana's marathon with several thousand participants.
• Festival Internacional de Jazz in Havana is Cuba's premier musical event with headliners line Chucho Valdez and other top acts from around the world.

December
• Festival Internacional de Nuevo Cinema draws film aficionados from all over the world. Havana's theaters are packed with locals and tourists for low priced, Latin American films.
• Most businesses close for Christmas day.

ETIQUETTE
Cubans are not as formal as many Latin Americans. Handshakes, formal greetings and the like are not the rule. Cubans are friendly and often touch you briefly on the hand, arm or shoulder when greeting.

Ladies: don't cover up!
Cuban women love short shorts, sexy tops and, although now disappearing, loudly colored spandex. They tend to dress very revealingly. If you, as a tourist, do the same, expect Cuban men to look over your assets and make audible comments. This is normal. In fact, if you dress conservatively they will probably do the same thing but you will be encouraging them if you dress sexy.

When boarding a bus or sitting down in a crowded restaurant it is nice to say "*buenas*" to those around you. This isn't done in the US but, in Cuba, people may think you are stuck up if you don't at least smile and acknowledge their presence. In general, people in Cuba are quite friendly to strangers. It is normal to strike up a casual conversation with seatmates or others around you. This is good: you can ask questions of the locals you encounter without feeling too nosey.

When beginning a meal or if you encounter someone already eating, it is polite to say "*buen provecho*," (have a nice meal).

FOOD & DINING
I have already mentioned that Cuba is not a fine dining destination. Most food offered to tourists is dreadful but better than what the locals are eating. Cuban food you may have eaten in Miami or other US towns is completely different from actual Cuban food on the island. Almost all Cuban food is bland. It is never spicy—in fact, you may have trouble finding salt and pepper.

Tourists will find chicken, pork and seafood pasta and pizza are common. Lobster is offered to tourists but it is illegal for Cubans to buy it, sell it or eat it. In Cuba, the famous Cuban sandwich consists of a small soft roll filled with spam—really. I have been served spam sandwiches on Cubana flights. White bread with mayonnaise (only mayonnaise) is a common sandwich sold on the street. Slices of crummy pizza are also common. Ice cream and coffee are usually safe bets. A few of the big hotels have decent restaurants. I can think of none I would call "good."

Most of the all-inclusive resorts have breakfast, lunch and dinner buffets. Most visitors are disappointed with what they find. Undercooked, over-cooked, spoiled, cold when it should be hot and hot when it should be cold is the norm. The resorts' a-la-carte restaurants where you need to make a reservation gen-erally have exactly the same food that is on the buffets but it is brought to your table by wait-ers—who expect a tip.

One notable exception to this is the food at some of the fishing lodges. If you are lucky enough to visit one of Avalon's lodges, you can expect wonderful fresh fish at every meal. You can eat lobster to your heart's content.

Almost all restaurants are government-owned and offer very low quality food. There is no incentive for employees to cook or serve well and farmers have little incentive to grow anything. The distribution systems are dysfunctional. According to some, employees steal as much as a third of food products in Cuba before it reaches restaurants or stores. There is a thriving black market. Even limes can be hard to find. Many bars and resorts do not serve mojitos due to lack of the hallmark ingredient: yerba buena (mint).

The government allows a few families to operate *paladars*, small restaurants in their homes. These are almost always good to excellent. I list a selection of these in each chapter where they are available. I manage to choke down watery eggs and toast at my hotel for breakfast and eat all my other meals at paladars if possible.

FURTHER READING
Field Guide to the Birds of Cuba
Orlando Garrido, Arturo Kirkconnell, Roman Company, (August, 2000).

Perelman's Pocket Cyclopedia of Havana Cigars
Richard B. Perelman, (1998).

Cuba Classics: A Celebration of Vintage American Automobiles
Christopher Baker, Interlink Books, (2004).

Hemingway in Cuba
Norberto Fuentes, Lyle Stuart, (1984).

Cuba Confidential
Ann Louise Bardach, Random House, (2002).

Havana Nocturne: How the Mob Owned Cuba and then Lost It to the Revolution
T.J. English, William Morrow, (2008).

Our Man in Havana
Graham Greene, Penguin, (1971).

Mi Moto Fidel: Motorcycling through Castro's Cuba
Christopher Baker, National Geographic Press, (2001).

HOTELS & LODGING
All hotels in Cuba are owned by the government and are often run in partnership with large international hotel chains with the Cuban government owning 51% and the foreign investors 49%. Pay no attention to Cuba's star rating system. No matter what they say, there are no five star hotels in Cuba. The best hotel in the country by far is the Parque Central in Havana and it barely ranks four stars in my opinion. The problems are poor food, terrible service and lack of everyday maintenance.

There are six Cuban government hotel chains. **Islazul** has properties targeted towards Cuban nationals and they are usually of the lowest quality. **Cubanacán** has what they call 4- and 5-star hotels, with a concentration in Havana, Varadero, Santa Lucía, Guardalavaca, Granma, and Santiago de Cuba. Their brands are Brisas, Club Amigo, Horizontes and, Cubanacan Hostales. **Gran Caribe** has what they consider 5-star hotels in Havana, Varadero and Cayo Largo. **Gaviota** operates 3- and 4-star properties in Varadero, Sancti Spíritus and Guardalavaca. **Horizontes** has 3-star hotels, with properties in Pinar del Río, Havana, Playas del Este, Matanzas, Varadero, Cienfuegos, Sancti Spíritus, Camagüey and Holguín. The best chain is **Habaganeaux** which has developed what they call boutique hotels in Old Havana. They do a fair job and I try to pick their hotels whenever possible.

It is important to know that the hotels charge the top prices if you simply walk in and ask for a room—without exception. If you book from outside the country you can usually get the rooms for about half the "rack" rate. If you book within Cuba you can usually get a better deal if you book from an agent from another hotel. The hotels will tell you this themselves. Several times I have been told to go across the street to another hotel to book the one I am asking at.

INTERNET ACCESS
The internet is not generally available to average Cubans. Many hotels have internet rooms guests can use. Wi-Fi (pronounced *wee-fee*) is relatively rare. Connections are very slow and you may find certain sites blocked. You can buy scratch-off internet access cards at most tourist hotels.

LANGUAGE
Cubans speak Spanish kind of like the way Jamaicans speak English (well, maybe not *that* bad). It can be a challenge for even fluent Spanish speakers to understand the local lingo. Locals tend to drop consonants and make up improbable contractions. "*Da me un pi de que*" would more properly be "*da me un pizza de queso*" give me a cheese pizza. "*Decu*" is short for *discúlpame*, excuse me. My Spanish is what I call "good" but it takes me a week or more to adapt my ear whenever I visit Cuba and I still have trouble. Fortunately, Cubans are almost all well educated and will understand you perfectly if you speak in reasonably correct, high school Spanish. Many, many Cubans speak at least a little English.

NEWSPAPERS & MAGAZINES
Even though it is dreadfully boring, you should get a few Cuban pesos and buy a copy of the national paper *Granma*. It is the main party organ and

contains mostly political diatribes, often written by El Líder, Castro. Locals buy it and some even read it. Since it is cheaper than toilet paper, many locals buy it for that reason alone. At least it has results and schedules for baseball games.

MAPS

There are several decent road maps available. The most common one is actually a tourist map that is so full of tiny little markings for the various sites that it can hardly be read at all. The best one to get is the plastic-coated published by **Nelles**. You can buy one from Amazon. Cuban road maps can have erroneous information. To foil the Yankee invader, some show non-existent roads and place towns in the wrong locations.

POSTAL SERVICE

At the time of this writing the USA did not accept any mail from Cuba. You can mail postcards from your hotel.

TIME

Cuba enjoys Eastern Standard Time, five hours behind Greenwich and changes for Daylight Savings.

TIPPING

Very few Cubans make more than a dollar or two a day — basically starvation wages, and rely on somehow cadging a few pesos here and there to get by. Even simple jobs in the tourist industry are highly prized since tips may happen. I feel sorry for them and tend to tip more in Cuba than I do in other countries and at home—*but only if I receive good service.* I round up to the nearest whole amount or add at least 10%.

Unfortunately, in Cuba, service is often extremely poor. Waiters seem to intentionally ignore you and can slam the plates down on your table while gazing off into the distance and never bring any silverware. Frequently you will need to get up from your table and go and find a waiter and ask them to come and take your order. You may need to do the same thing if you want more coffee or are ready to pay your bill. In stores, because the government owns the stores and there is no incentive for anyone to actually do any work or be helpful to customers, staff will sometimes ignore you completely hoping you will just leave.

Most employees earn less than $25 a month and many do not get to choose their jobs. Even though almost any job in tourism is valued, many waiters never decided to be waiters—the government told them that's what they will be for life. Obviously, this can lead to rude and indifferent service.

At many places, a tip is included in the bill. Before tipping, check to see if a tip is included in your bill. The government receives all the proceeds, including tips and pays staff only their regular, miniscule wages. If it is on the bill, the waiter will probably not get it. So I will often leave a few pesos on the table in addition to whatever tip the government plans on glomming from the poor waiter. I also leave a peso or two on my pillow for the maids who clean my room. Sad? Unfair to both customers and staff? Yes, but that's Cuba.

Tipping At All-inclusive Resorts
My advice is: tip early and tip frequently. At many of the all-inclusive

resorts, service staff will let you know you can expect dreadful service if you do not tip. Often, at the beginning of your stay, service is good but gets progressively worse as the week goes by if you do not tip on a daily basis. Guests are instructed to leave a large tip at the end of their stay presumably to be divided by the entire staff. *Do not do this.* The government gets this money—*the staff does not.* If you tip the guy making omelets or doing the shrimp stir-fry, you will get faster service, a nicer omelet or more shrimp. If you do not, expect to stand around for while the cook slowly takes care of everyone else and then gets your order wrong. He is trying to tell you something: leave a tip. I approach the buffets with a peso visible in my hand.

TOURIST INFORMATION
Infotur
Tel. 537-866-3333; www.infotur.cu

TRAVEL AGENCIES
Cubanacán
Tel. 537-204-4756; www.cubanacanviajes.com

Cubatur
Tel. 537-835-4155; www.cubatur.cu

Gaviota Tours
Tel. 537-209-4528; www.gaviota-grupo.com

Paradiso
Tel. 537-832-9538; www.paradiso.cu

WATER
Drinking water from the tap is not a good idea in most places. Some hotels filter their tap water or offer guests purified water (*agua mineral* or *agua pura*) in their rooms. Most tourist bars that are nice enough to have ice will use purified water to make it.

WEBSITES
Tripadvisor (*www.tripadvisor.com*) is one of the very best sites for itinerary planning. The forums are full of comments from travelers about their experiences with hotels, restaurants and tour operators, and how their itineraries worked out. Post your questions and you are likely to get useful answers from people who have just come back. A great site.

Another good site to hang around and get travel information at is **Lonely Planet** (*Info: www.lonelyplanet.com/cuba*). Their forums and reviews are especially helpful.

WEIGHTS & MEASURES
Cuba, like many countries, is inching over to the metric system. Fuel is sold by the liter. Road signs and speed limits are in kilometers.

WHAT TO BRING
Some toiletry items are difficult to find in Cuba. Things like sunscreen, condoms, hats, bubba mugs, and aspirin are better bought at home. You can buy sunscreen in Cuba but the selection will be poor and the price high. I am not a big believer in bringing gift items to Cuba to hand out. I do like to bring some small items to give to friends. Simple medical and personal hygiene supplies like aspirin, Band-Aids, toothpaste, etc. are in very short supply in Cuba and Cubans are pleased to receive them.

Although probably forbidden, I also like to bring packets of vegetable seeds as gifts. Most recipients seem more pleased by these than any other gifts I bring. By doing this I also hope to improve the extremely bland Cuban cuisine overall with the hot pepper seeds I bring. Perhaps they will catch on. Many people appreciate packs of fishhooks and I sometimes bring guitar strings for my musician friends.

Visitors to all-inclusive beach and buffet resorts who like to drink by the pool or on the beach often bring their own insulated "bubba" mugs to fill up at the bar and take back to their lounge chair. Good idea and almost all the resort bars are happy to give you a good double or triple shot of your favorite tipple. To encourage bartender enthusiasm in this, a small tip should work well.

ESSENTIAL SPANISH

Pleasantries

A simple "*buenas*" works just fine for a casual "hello" or "goodbye" almost any time of day, but it is more polite to come out with the whole salutation: *buenos días, buenas tardes* or *buenas noches*.

Please – *por favor*
Thank you – *gracias*
You're welcome – *de nada*
Excuse me – *perdóneme, permiso or discúlpeme*
Good day – *buenos días*
Good night – *buenas noches*
Goodbye – *adiós*
Hello – *hola*
How are you? – *¿Cómo está Usted?* or *¿Qué tal?*
Fine – *muy bien*
Pleased to meet you – *mucho gusto*

Everyday Phrases

Yes – *sí*
No – *no*
I don't know. – *No sé.*
Do you speak English? – *¿Habla usted inglés?*
I don't speak Spanish. – *Yo no hablo español.*
Friend – *amigo*
Where? – *¿Dónde?*
When? – *¿Cuando?*
Why? – *¿Porqué?*
Because – *por qué*
How much? – *¿Cuanto?*
How do you say…? – *¿Cómo se dice…?*
Today – *hoy*
Tomorrow – *mañana*
Yesterday – *ayer*
I would like – *quisiera*
Here – *aquí*
There – *allá*
More – *más*
Less – *menos*
Much – *mucho*

Little – *poco*
Large – *grande*
Small – *pequeño*
Good – *bueno*
Bad – *malo*

Travel Terms
Airport – *(el) aeropuerto*
ATM – *cajeras automáticas*
Avenue – *(la) Avenida*
Bank – *(el) banco*
Bathroom – *(el) baño, sanitario*
Boat – *(el) barco, bote, lancha*
Bus – *(el) autobús, camioneta*
Car – *(el) coche, carro*
Front desk – *(la) carpeta*
Gas station – *(la) bomba, gasolinera*
Hotel – *(el) hotel*
How far is . . . ¿ – *¿Qué distancia es. . . ?*
Lookout point - *mirador*
Money – *(el) dinero*
Taxi – *(el) taxi*
Road, highway – *(la) carretera*
Street – *(la) calle*

Eating & Drinking
Apple – *(la) manzana*
Banana – *(el) banano*
Barbeque – *(la) parilla*
Beef – *(el) bistec*
Beer – *(la) cerveza*
Black coffee – *café negro, café natural*
Bottled water – *agua mineral or agua pura*
Bread – *(el) pan*
Cheese – *(el) queso*
Chicken – *(el) pollo*
Coffee – *(el) café*
Coffee with milk – *café con leche*
Cuban food – comida criolla
Delicious – *delicioso*

Drunk – *borracho*
Fish – *(el) pescado*
Fruits – *(las) frutas*
Garlic – (el) ajo
Glass of water – *un vaso de agua*
Glass of wine – *una copa de vino*
Guacamole – *(el) guacamol*
Guava – *(la) guayaba*
Ham – *(el) jamón*
Have a nice meal – *buen provecho*
Juice – *(el) jugo*
Lemon, lime – *(el) limón*
Liver – *(el) hígado*
Marinated seafood salad – *(el) ceviche*
Meat – *(la) carne*
Menu – *(el) menú, lista*
Milk – *(la) leche*
Octopus – *(el) pulpo*
Orange – *(la) naranja*
Papaya – *fruta bomba* (*not papaya* which refers to female genitalia)
Pineapple – *(la) piña*
Plantain – *(el) plátano*
Pork – *(el) cerdo*

INDEX

AIRPORTS 12-13, 91, 112, 114, 142-143, 152
ATMs 149, 166

BANKS 149
Barracuda Diving Center 73
Baseball 29, 41, 59, 95, 160
Beaches 9-10, 12-14, 18-19, 26, 30, 32, 60-61, 63, 65-66, 68, 71-72, 77, 83, 91-92, 98-99, 102-106, 108, 112, 114-116, 118-119, 123, 130, 137, 139, 164
Beer 22, 77, 105
Bello Bar 86
Birding 25, 30, 89, 110, 121, 128, 136, 139-140
Blau Colonial Hotel 99
Blau Varadero Hotel 67
Blue Bay Cayo Coco 99
Bodegon Criollo 70
Bodeguita del Medio 28, 54
Bus 39, 148
Bus Tour 39
Business hours 150

CAR RENTAL 145
Carnival 10, 77, 80, 85, 155
Casa 1932 45
Casa Alejandro Thomas 83
Casa Antigua 44
Casa Colonial Mercedes 135
Casa Dania 46
Casa de La Mœsica 14, 56, 58, 87
Casa de La Trova 27, 76-78, 86-87
Casa de Los Estudiantes 87
Casa El Porry 130, 175
Casa Evora 45

Casa Habana Lourdes 48
Casa Leonardo y Rosa 83
Casa Ony y Luis 135
Casa Vilma y Peter 83
Casas Particulares 18, 21, 42, 65
Catamaran Cruise 74
Cayo Coco 12, 23, 31, 88, 91-92, 98-100, 105-110
Cayo Guillermo 92-94, 100-102, 105-110
Cayo Largo 13, 24-26, 31-32, 60, 111-121, 159
Cayo Levisa 14, 32, 130, 138-141
Cayo Santa Mar'a 94-99, 102
Cell Phones 151
Cigars 15, 39, 130, 143, 152, 158
Climate 17, 136, 150
Club 300, 86
Club Amigo Carisol Los Corales 83
Club Salseando Chevere 59
Coffee 16, 21, 53
Copelia 40, 69
Credit Cards 149
Crime 153
Cruises 143
Cubacar 146

DIVING 13, 25, 30-32, 24-25, 31, 68, 72, 73, 88, 106-108, 117, 119, 123-135, 137-140
Driving 144-145
Drug stores 154
Drugs 55

EL FLORIDITA 28, 54
El Gringo Viejo 53
El Morro 79, 84

El Pueblo La Estrella 105
El Quitrín 85
El Templete 35, 50
Electricity 152
Embassies 151
Emergencies 153
Etiquette 156

FISHING 13, 23-24, 30-32, 59-60, 65, 73-74, 89, 108-110, 112, 114, 120, 123, 127-128

GALER'A SANTIAGO 85
Gato Tuerto 55, 56
Golf 29, 59, 75
Gran Caribe Club Bucanero 82
Guardalavaca 12-13, 91, 103-104, 106-110
Guayaberas 16-17

HAVANA 9, 10, 12, 15-18, 28-29, 30, 32, 33-61, 65, 142-156, 158-159
Havanautos 146
Health 154
Hemingway, Ernest 28-29, 38, 54, 91, 158
Hospitals 154
Hostal Los Frailes 45
Hotel Brisas Guardalavaca 104
Hotel Casa Granda Santiago de Cuba 77, 81
Hotel Cayo Levisa 139
Hotel Nacional 50
Hotel Playa Blanca (Gran Caribe) 116
Hotel Plaza 44
Hotel San Basilio 82
Hotel Saratoga 44
Hotel Tortuga 123, 125
Hurricanes 43, 151

IBEROSTAR DAIQUIRI 100
Iberostar Ensenachos 102
Iberostar Tainos 69
Iberostar Varadero 66

Il Diluvio 51
Inglaterra 43

JARDINES DE LA REINA 13, 24, 25, 122-128
Jardines del Rey 12
Jazz 28, 55, 56, 57, 49, 155, 156
Jazz Cafe 28, 55, 57
Jeep Safari 63, 92

LA CAMPANA 70
La Cocina de Lilliam 52
La Comparsita 72
La Cueva de Los Indios 132
La Ermita 132, 134
La Guarida 48, 49
La Maison 88
La Zorra y El Cuervo 57
Lai Lai 70
Language 160
Las Gallegas Paladar 84
Los Jazmines 154

MALECÓN 15, 24, 33-35, 60
Mambo Club 71
Maps 161
Mar'a La Gorda 14, 25, 30, 130, 137-139
Marina Gaviota 73
Meliá Buena Vista 102
Meliá Cayo Coco 98
Meliá Cayo Guillermo 101
Meliá Cohiba 48
Meliá Santiago de Cuba 82
Money 149
Museo de La Mœsica 39
Museo del Chocolate 38
Museo del Ron 39, 80
Museo Emilio Bacardi 80
Museo Hemingway 38
Museum of the Revolution 35

NATIONAL FINE ARTS MUSEUM 38
Necropolis Cristobal Colon 39-40

Newspapers 160
NH Krystal Laguna Villas & Resort 100
Nightlife 44, 53-59, 71-72, 85-88, 106, 118, 136
Northern Cays 90-110

OCCIDENTAL MIRAMAR 47

PALADAR CASA DON TOMAS 135
Paladar Nieto 50
Panautos 146
Paradisus Princesa del Mar 65
Paradisus Río de Oro Resort & Spa 103-104
Partagas Cigar Factory 39
Pizza Nova 69
Playas del Este 61
Postal Service 161
Prostitution 57

ROYAL HIDEAWAY ENSENACHOS: see Iberostar Ensenachos
Rum 16, 22, 39, 69, 80

SALÓN ROSADA BENY MOR 14
Sandals Royal Hicacos Resort 68
Santiago 10, 68, 76-89
Saturno Cave 63
Shopping 15-17, 53, 70, 84-85, 105-106, 118, 136, 143
Skydiving 75
Sol Cayo Coco 90, 98

Sol Cayo Guillermo 101
Sol Cayo Largo 115
Sol Pelícano 116
Sol Río De Luna y Mares 104
Snorkeling 24-25, 72-73, 88-89, 106-108, 119, 126-127, 138, 140
Surfing 23

TALLER DE CERAMICA ARTISTICA 70
Taxis 146, 147
Thomas Cook 95-96
Time 161
Tipping 109, 162
Train Station 148
Travel Agencies 163
Tropicana 58, 72, 87
Tryp Cayo Coco 100

VARADERO 10, 54, 62-75
Villa Cabo San Antonio 137
Villa María La Gorda Gaviota 138
Villa Marinera 117
Villa Pupi y Norma 135
Villa Tito y Janet 134
Viñales 14, 130-136
Vistamar 52

WEATHER 150
Western Cuba 14, 30-31, 129-141
Wine 22

ZUNZUN 84

THINGS CHANGE!

Phone numbers, prices, addresses, quality of service – all change. If you come across any new information, let us know. No item is too small! Contact us at :

jopenroad@aol.com

or

www.openroadguides.com

TravelNotes

TravelNotes

PHOTO CREDITS

All maps are by Bruce Morris.

The following photos are from Bruce Morris: pp. 31, 32, 40, 60, 90, 99 top.
The following photos are from Cuban Diving Centers/Cuban Fishing Centers (cubandivingcenters.com; cubanfishingcenters.com): pp. 117, 119, 120, 125, 127. *The following photo is from Seamus Harris* (bunnyhugs.org): p. 51.

The following photos are from wikimedia commons: p. 26: Kirua; p. 28: Scewing; p. 75: Marek Silarski; p. 76: Petrusbarbygere; p. 81 DirkvdM; p. 107: Instituto Argentino de Buceo; p. 11: Vgenecr; p. 118: Panther.

The following images are from flickr.com: front cover photo: Mikelo; back cover photo and pp. 7, 173: Iker Merodio; pp. 1, 3: liee_wu; p. 6: jon crel; pp. 8, 34: Marc Veraart; p. 9: cubanjunky; p. 12: flippinyank; pp. 13, 121: topyti; p. 14: samurai_dave; p. 15: juicylucymamma; p. 19: Avodrocc; p. 21: Numinosity; pp. 25, 74: Phil Guest; p. 27: hoyasmeg; p. 33: motumboe; pp. 36, 162, 164. 167: *christopher*; p. 38: Zambog; p. 41: boomer-44; p. 56: Paul Turgeon; p. 58: jennicatpink; p. 61: ilkerender; pp. 62, 147: Dani Figueiredo; p. 86: marek.krzystkiewicz; p. 87: Boggin; p. 89: Dominic Sherony; p. 92: O. Taillon; p. 94: jodastephen; p. 95: neiljs; p. 96: Space Ritual; p. 110: Igooch; pp. 122, 128: dMap Travel Guide; pp. 129, 137, 141: Geoffroy M.; p. 132: fraufrida; pp. 133, 152: Matt Dowdeswell; p. 143: NatalieMaynor; p. 144: Mike_fleming; p. 145: mirandalovestraveling; p. 149: douglemoine; p. 150: Effervescing Elephants; p. 155: Leshaines 123; p. 157: hellosputnik; p. 159: Stuart_Burns1; p. 160: syue2k; p. 161: Fiat-Black 66.

Note: the use of these photos does not represent an endorsement of this book or any services listed within by any of the photographers listed above.

Open Road Publishing

Open Road has launched a greatl new concept in travel guides that we call our *Best Of* guides: matching the time you *really* have for your vacation with the right amount of information you need for your perfect trip! No fluff, just the best things to do and see, the best places to stay and eat. Includes one-day, weekend, one-week and two-week trip ideas. Now what could be more perfect than that?

Best Of Guides

Open Road's Best of Arizona, $12.95
Open Road's Best of The Florida Keys & Everglades, $12.95
Open Road's Best of Las Vegas, $14.95
Open Road's Best of New York City, $14.95
Open Road's Best of Southern California, $14.95
Open Road's Best of Northern California, $14.95
Open Road's Best of The Bahamas, $14.95
Open Road's Best of Bermuda, $14.95
Open Road's Best of Belize, $14.95
Open Road's Best of Cuba, $12.95
Open Road's Best of Costa Rica, $12.95
Open Road's Best of Panama, $12.95
Open Road's Best of Guatemala, $9.95
Open Road's Best of Italy, $14.95
Open Road's Best of Paris, $12.95
Open Road's Best of Provence & The French Riviera, $12.95
Open Road's Best of Spain, $14.95

Family Travel Guides

Open Road's Italy with Kids, $14.95
Open Road's Paris with Kids, $16.95
Open Road's Caribbean with Kids, $14.95
Open Road's London with Kids, $12.95
Open Road's Best National Parks With Kids, $12.95
Open Road's Washington, DC with Kids, $14.95